QuickCook

QuickCook
Fish

Recipes by Emma Lewis

Every dish, three ways—you choose!
30 minutes | 20 minutes | 10 minutes

An Hachette UK Company
www.hachette.co.uk

First published in Great Britain in 2012 by Hamlyn,
a division of Octopus Publishing Group Ltd.
Endeavour House, 189 Shaftesbury Avenue
London WC2H 8JY UK
www.octopusbooks.co.uk

Distributed in the U.S. by Hachette Book Group USA,
237 Park Avenue, New York NY 10017 USA
www.octopusbooksusa.com

Distributed in Canada by Canadian Manda Group,
165 Dufferin Street, Toronto, Ontario, Canada M6K 3H6

Recipes by Emma Lewis
Copyright © Octopus Publishing Group Ltd 2012

ISBN 978-0-60062-404-2

Printed and bound in China

10 9 8 7 6 5 4 3 2

Ovens should be preheated to the specified temperature. If using a convection oven,
follow the manufacturer's instructions for adjusting the time and temperature.
Broilers should also be preheated.

This book includes dishes made with nuts and nut derivatives. It is advisable for
those with known allergic reactions to nuts and nut derivatives and those who may
be potentially vulnerable to these allergies, such as pregnant and nursing mothers,
invalids, the elderly, babies, and children, to avoid dishes made with nuts and nut oils.
It is also prudent to check the labels of pre-prepared ingredients for the possible
inclusion of nut derivatives.

Eggs should not be consumed raw. This book contains some dishes made with raw
or lightly cooked eggs. It is prudent for more vulnerable people such as pregnant and
nursing mothers, invalids, the elderly, babies, and young children to avoid uncooked
or lightly cooked dishes made with eggs.

Contents

Introduction

30 20 10—Quick, Quicker, Quickest

This book offers a new and flexible approach to meal-planning for busy cooks, letting you choose the recipe option that best fits the time you have available. Inside you will find 360 dishes that will inspire and motivate you to get cooking every day of the year. All the recipes take a maximum of 30 minutes to cook. Some take as little as 20 minutes and, amazingly, many take only 10 minutes. With a bit of preparation, you can easily try out one new recipe from this book each night and slowly you will be able to build a wide and exciting portfolio of recipes to suit your needs.

How Does it Work?

Every recipe in the QuickCook series can be cooked one of three ways—a 30-minute version, a 20-minute version, or a super-quick and easy 10-minute version. At the beginning of each chapter you'll find recipes listed by time. Choose a dish based on how much time you have and turn to that page.

You'll find the main recipe in the middle of the page accompanied by a beautiful photograph, as well as two time-variation recipes below.

If you enjoy your chosen dish, why not go back and cook the other time-variation options at a later date? So if you've tried and liked the 20-minute Smoked Haddock and Corn Chowder, but only have 10 minutes to spare this time around, you'll find a way to cook the same flavors in a different recipe using quick ingredients or clever shortcuts.

If you love the ingredients and flavors of the 10-minute Prosciutto, Scallop, and Rosemary Skewers, why not try something more substantial, like the 20-minute Scallop, Chorizo, and Rosemary Stew, or be inspired to make a more elaborate version, like the Scallops with Rosemary Risotto? Alternatively, browse through all 360 delicious recipes, find something that catches your eye—then cook the version that fits your time frame.

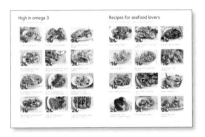

Or, for easy inspiration, turn to the gallery on pages 12–19 to get an instant overview by themes, such as High in Omega 3 or Recipes for Seafood Lovers.

QuickCook online

To make life even easier, you can use the special code on each recipe page to email yourself a recipe card for printing, or email a text-only shopping list to your phone. Go to www.hamlynquickcook.com and enter the recipe code at the bottom of each page.

FIS-FAMI-QAR

Fast Fish

With little time to spare, many of us are looking for easier ways to prepare a meal. It's tempting to reach for a takeout menu or fast-forward to the "ping" of a microwave, but these catering solutions often don't offer value for money, nor are they reliably nutritious. Home cooking wins on both these counts and yet it doesn't have to be elaborate or time-consuming, especially if you choose fish. As well as being very good for you, which is why we are all advised to eat it twice a week, fish cooks incredibly quickly. Many fish dishes take no longer than 10 minutes to rustle up—in fact, because of its delicate flesh, fish is at its best when cooked only briefly.

Tooling up

Anyone who likes cooking fish should invest in a large, heavy nonstick skillet, which is perfect for cooking thin fish fillets in a flash. Chunkier fillets of firm-fleshed fish will benefit greatly from being cooked on a ridged griddle pan, giving your fish an appealing smoky, barbecue-like taste. Poaching is a subtle and healthy way of cooking fish, but choose a large, shallow pan for this method, which will also be suitable for steaming. For broiling and roasting fish, a large roasting pan is ideal for cooking several fish fillets at once when you don't have much time, or for cooking a whole fish for a special occasion. If you can't resist a piece of deep-fried fish, make sure you have a large, deep saucepan to hold enough oil for deep-frying, and a thermometer, which is useful for checking the oil temperature.

Stocking up

Fish has a wonderful, unique, delicate flavor. You can serve it really simply with just a squeeze of fresh lemon juice or scatter some fresh herbs and a little butter on top. But it also tastes good teamed with punchy flavors, so keep jars of olives, capers, and cornichons in your kitchen cupboard for an instant piquant accompaniment or stir them through mayonnaise for an easy condiment. Chunkier sauces like pesto and salsa also go well with fish, while a handful of bread crumbs scattered on top and crisped up under a broiler is a hit with kids. You can't store fresh fish for very long, but canned fish is invaluable to have around. Tuna is a firm favorite for most families and, like canned salmon, is endlessly versatile—try it stirred into pasta, made into a fishcake or simply served as salad. Anchovies won't satisfy the appetite, but a couple of them added to a sauce or dressing will immediately bring a richness to the flavor. Fish can be frozen, but the texture does suffer in the process. Seafood, however, is fine for freezing. Shrimp, for example, make a wonderful last-minute meal cooked with frozen peas in a risotto, and squid and scallops are also worthwhile candidates for the freezer.

Shopping for fish

Fish is widely available in supermarkets these days, and many of the larger stores have dedicated fish counters offering a great selection of fresh produce. You may also be fortunate enough to have a fish dealer nearby. It's worth tracking down one of these gems, because the staff are so knowledgeable about the different types of fish on offer, and are able to expertly clean, fillet, and present it as well as provide you with plenty of tips on cooking. They can also talk you through the issues of fish sustainability—as our enjoyment of fish has increased, a number of species have been overfished and are now protected. Seafood can be quite expensive, and turbot or lobster is probably best enjoyed as a special treat. But with a little shopping around, you'll find fish that's affordable enough to be eaten everyday. Try using relatively inexpensive sea robin or yellow perch in place of pricier cod and haddock, while rainbow trout is a dependable all-round fish and salmon can be a surprising bargain. Mackerel and sardines are not only packed full of essential oils and vitamins, they are also really cost-effective choices. If you like seafood, shrimp are often good value and a few of the larger variety go a long way, while clams and mussels are often cheaper than you might expect.

Choosing the right fish

People are often a bit squeamish about buying fish and worried about how to choose the freshest possible. You can tell a lot from the appearance of a fish—look for bright, fresh eyes and a clear skin. Fillets and steaks should also have clear-colored skin, be firm to the touch (not breaking apart) and, contrary to what some might think, no fish should smell fishy when it's bought. The classic smell that can turn people off eating fish comes from decomposition, so any fishy fish are best avoided! It's sometimes a little overwhelming looking at a fish counter offering a wide selection of fish. Where do you start if you've never cooked fish before? What will all the family enjoy eating? What will make a really impressive dinner? The following guide will help you to understand the different types of fish available.

Classic white fish

Flaky white fish such as cod, haddock, halibut, pollock, and whiting (also called silver hake) are the most popular options. They don't have an overpowering taste, are low in fat and make a safe choice if you are unsure about eating fish. You can interchange any of these fish in the recipes in this book, depending on what is available in the supermarket and the size of your budget. They are quick to cook and very versatile— you'll find nice thick fillets, or chunky steaks that are great to cook speedily under the broiler or that can be sliced into thin strips and added to a stew or stir-fry. Just make sure you don't cook the fish too long, or it will break apart into flakes.

Dependable salmon and tuna

For those who think they don't like fish, or would prefer to eat meat, robust and flavorful salmon and tuna are your best options. Salmon is probably the most versatile fish of all—you can prepare and cook salmon steaks or fillets in a wide variety of ways, or cut it into chunks for stews, mince it for a child-friendly dish or serve a whole salmon for entertaining. Fresh tuna is normally sold as steaks and needs only the briefest of cooking—like a fine piece of beefsteak, the center should be ruby rare, so literally a minute or two under the broiler is all it needs. Salmon should be cooked through but again doesn't need long or it will lose its natural moist texture.

Fish packed full of essential oils

To reduce the risk of heart disease, it's recommended that we eat at least one portion of oily fish a week to reap the benefits of all the healthy fish oils. Salmon is packed full of these oils, as is fresh (but not canned) tuna. But you might also like to try mackerel, which has lots of flavor and is great in a curry, the smaller sardine or, that Scandinavian favorite, the herring.

Something a bit more adventurous

More uncommon and a little higher in price are white fish such as sea bass and sea bream (scup). These fish are a real treat when cooked whole but are also good cut into fillets and served with a flavorful sauce if you are short of time. For something sturdier in texture, look for monkfish (monkfish tail is sometimes known as "poor man's lobster"). The robust flesh of swordfish makes it the perfect choice for threading onto skewers to cook on the barbecue. Halibut, which comes in enormous steaks, is another foolproof firm fish and is great in a curry. Squid and scallops take just a minute or so to cook and will give any dish the "Wow!" factor. Their flesh is sturdy and dense enough to stand up to some feisty cooking methods—they are both well-suited to being deep-fried or stewed—but their delicate yet distinctive flavors also lend themselves to being quickly fried and then simply served with a wedge of lemon on the side. There are many more exotic fish available from fisheries around the world—among these, hoki, red snapper, and tilapia are all tasty white fish that you will come across from time to time and are well worth sampling.

Fish to impress

A whole fish presented on a serving platter is guaranteed to impress for a special meal. Flatfish tend to fall apart when stewed, so are best cut into fillets and simply cooked or left whole. Turbot and Dover sole are the kings of this type of fish and are much admired by chefs, but they are expensive and hard to obtain sometimes. So, for something just a bit out of the ordinary for a weekday, try American plaice or lemon sole, which are both a type of flounder. Once thought of as the ultimate luxury, some shellfish and crustaceans can now be surprisingly affordable, and you often need only a relatively small quantity to make an impact. Shrimp are widely available, don't cost a fortune, and are good for freezing. Look for larger plump varieties, and for maximum flavor, keep the shell on. Langoustine and lobsters are for special occasions only, but their plump sweet flesh makes a truly memorable treat. Clams and mussels are ideal for entertaining on a budget—they may be slightly unusual to look at but are simple to cook and great value for money.

12 Ways With Salmon

Deliciously different recipes for salmon-lovers

Corn Cakes with Smoked Salmon 52

Honey Mustard Salmon 82

Proper Salmon Fishcakes with Dill Sauce 84

Salmon Tikka Masala 90

Crispy Salmon and Pesto Parcels 98

Salmon, Pea, and Dill Tortilla 106

Smoked Salmon Sushi Salad 194

Roasted Salmon with Peach Salsa 216

Crispy Rice Paper Salmon Parcels with Soy Dressing 234

Smoked Salmon and Beet Salad with Creamy Dressing 244

Confit Salmon with Watercress Salad 248

Hot-Smoked Salmon Kedgeree with Quails' Eggs 258

Pasta, Noodles, and Rice

Filling recipes with a fish twist

Smoked Trout Pasta with Creamy Dill Sauce 44

Seafood Risotto 62

Simple Tuna Pasta 110

Salmon and Leek Cannelloni 118

New Orleans Jambalaya 120

Shrimp Laksa 132

Seafood Paella 134

Leek and Smoked Haddock Risotto 142

Pad Thai 172

Tuna Soba Noodles with Ponzu Dressing 186

Creamy Seafood Lasagne 260

Clam Linguine in Chile Crème Fraîche Sauce 276

Soups, Stews, and Pot Pies

Easy recipes for winter days

Chinese Crab and Sweetcorn Soup 34

Trout and Bacon Hash 80

Smoked Haddock and Corn Chowder 86

Fish Pie 114

Spicy Peanut and Fish Stew 148

Monkfish, Chorizo, and Chickpea Stew 156

Asian Fishball Soup 220

Bouillabaisse 232

Shellfish and Tomato Bisque 278

Tomato and Fennel Fish Pie 196

Smoked Haddock Soufflé 240

Shrimp and Leek Pot Pies 254

Using the Whole Fish

Meals using whole fish that are sure to impress

Plaice Florentine 108

Lemon and Bacon-Wrapped Trout 146

Skate with Lemon Butter and Capers 150

Baked Sea Bream with Fennel 152

Baked Sea Bass with Romseco Salad 158

Sea Bream with Tomatoes and Basil 192

Couscous and White Fish Parcels 218

Chinese Banquet Sea Bass 246

Baked Turbot with a Buttery Tarragon Sauce 256

Whole Roasted Salmon with Lemon and Herb Tartare 264

Pan-Fried Sole with Butter and Lemon 266

Sea Bass Baked in Salt Crust with Fennel Mayo 272

High in Omega 3

Healthy dishes for all the family

Smoked Mackerel Pâté 32

Anchovy and Olive Crostini 38

Moroccan Sardine Pita Breads 48

Kipper Salad with Creamy Mustard Dressing 54

Mackerel Goujons with Sour cream and Paprika Dip 64

Crunchy Sardine Caesar Salad 92

Baked Mullet with Orange and Olive Couscous 128

Mackerel with Roasted Tomatoes and Horseradish 138

Halibut Ceviche with Grapefruit and Chiles 198

Smoked Trout, Cucumber, and Radish Salad 206

Oatmeal Herrings with Beet Salad 212

Broiled Mackerel with Lemon, Chile, and Cilantro 226

Recipes for Seafood Lovers

A selection of original recipes using shellfish and seafood

Italian Seafood Salad 24

Broiled Lemony Oysters with Spinach 40

Steamed Mussels in Wine 50

Crayfish Cocktail 56

Garlicky Shrimp and Sherry Tapas 66

Crispy Lemon Shrimp Skewers 102

Clams in Black Bean Sauce 140

Fruits de Mer with Herb Aïoli 242

Lobster Thermidor 262

Creamy Oysters and Mushrooms in Brioche Pots 268

Citrus Scallop Ceviche 270

Crispy Deep-Fried Seafood 274

Touch of Spice

Enjoy a taste of the East with these hot and spicy recipes

Salt and Pepper Squid Bites 46

Spicy Tuna Empanadas 88

Fish Tortillas with Avocado Salsa 112

Cajun-Blackened Fish Steaks 136

Hake with Spicy Cilantro Pesto 144

Tuna Teriyaki with Wasabi Mashed Potatoes 154

Peppered Tuna with Arugula and Parmesan 170

Steamed Sea Bream with Asian Flavors 180

Coconut Fish Curry 208

Spiced Fish Tagine 224

Crab Cakes with Chipotle Salsa 238

Chile Crab 252

Comfort Food

Indulge yourself with these comforting fish-flavored treats

Vietnamese Egg Rolls 28

Indian Shrimp Omelet Wraps 58

Best Crab Sandwich Ever 68

Mini Garlicky Cod Bites 70

Beer-Battered Cod and Chips 76

Asian Seafood Noodles 78

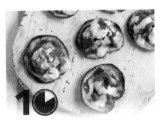

Mini Seafood Pizza Bites 94

Sweet and Sour Fish 100

Smoked Haddock Rarebit 122

Tuna Burgers with Mango Salsa 182

Healthy Fish Supper with Homemade Tomato Ketchup 190

Oven-Baked Thai Fishcakes 202

QuickCook

Light
Bites

Recipes listed by cooking time

10

 Italian Seafood Salad

Serves 4

¾ cup dry white wine
1 shallot, diced
1 lb cleaned live clams
5 oz raw peeled jumbo shrimp
6 cleaned large scallops
1 lemon
handful of basil, chopped
5 tablespoons extra virgin olive oil
¾ cup cherry tomatoes, halved
4 cups salad leaves
salt and pepper

- Bring the wine and shallot to a boil in a saucepan. Reduce the heat and add the clams. Cover the pan and cook for 5 minutes, or until the clams have opened. Discard any that remain closed. Transfer to a bowl using a slotted spoon and set aside to cool.

- Add the shrimp to the pan and cook for 1–2 minutes. Add the scallops and cook for a further 3 minutes, turning halfway through cooking, until the shrimp are pink and just cooked. Set the shrimp to one side and slice the scallops.

- Whisk together the finely grated zest of the lemon with a good squeeze of the juice, the basil, oil, and a little of the seafood cooking liquid. Season with salt and pepper and then toss the seafood in half the dressing.

- Arrange the tomatoes and salad leaves on serving plates. Place the seafood on top and drizzle with the remaining dressing to serve.

 Spicy Seafood Salad

Cook 3½ oz raw squid rings in hot water for 2 minutes. Drain and cool. Whisk together 1 crushed garlic clove, 1 minced red chile, 1 tablespoon fish sauce, a pinch of superfine sugar, and 1–2 teaspoons fresh lime juice. Toss with 4 oz cooked peeled jumbo shrimp, the squid, ¼ sliced cucumber, 1 sliced romaine lettuce, and a handful each cilantro and mint, chopped.

 Seafood Crêpes with Basil Sauce

Cook the seafood as above. Boil the cooking liquid until reduced to 3½ tablespoons. Stir in a scant ½ cup light cream, 1–2 teaspoons fresh lemon juice, and a handful of basil, chopped. Keep warm. Meanwhile, place 1 cup all-purpose flour in a bowl. Crack in 2 eggs, mix together, then slowly beat in 1¼ cups milk. Season. Heat a little olive oil in a nonstick skillet. Cook a ladleful of the batter for 30 seconds. Turn the crêpe over and cook for 30 seconds more until just cooked through. Transfer to a plate and keep warm. Repeat to make 6–8 crêpes. Stir the seafood into the sauce and use it to fill the crêpes. Pour a little of the sauce on top, scatter with extra chopped herbs, and serve.

 # Prosciutto, Scallop, and Rosemary Skewers

Serves 3–4

6 thin slices of prosciutto
12 cleaned large scallops
12 long, thick rosemary sprigs
3 tablespoons olive oil
salt

- Cut the prosciutto in half lengthwise. Wrap a piece around each scallop.

- Strip the leaves from the bottom of each rosemary sprig, then thread each scallop onto a rosemary "skewer."

- Drizzle with the oil and season with salt. Cook under a hot broiler or on a hot barbecue for 5 minutes, or until just cooked through, turning once.

 ### Scallop, Chorizo, and Rosemary

Stew Heat 1 tablespoon olive oil in a large saucepan. Cook 4 oz chorizo, cut into thick slices, for about 2 minutes, or until golden. Add 2 sliced garlic cloves and cook for 30 seconds. Stir in 1 teaspoon tomato paste followed by a scant ½ cup dry white wine and cook until nearly boiled off. Pour in a 13½ oz can diced tomatoes and add a sprig of rosemary. Bring to a boil, then simmer for 8 minutes, adding a little water if necessary. Stir in 12 cleaned plump scallops and cook for 2–3 minutes, or until just cooked through. Scatter with a handful of chopped flat-leaf parsley just before serving.

 ### Scallops with Rosemary Risotto

Heat 1 tablespoon olive oil in a large, deep skillet. Add 1 diced onion and cook for 5 minutes until softened, then add 1 crushed garlic clove and cook for a further 1 minute. Stir in 1½ cups risotto rice until well coated. Pour in ¼ cup dry white wine and 1 teaspoon finely chopped rosemary and boil until the wine has reduced. Add about 5 cups hot vegetable stock, a ladleful at a time, stirring and simmering after each addition until the stock is absorbed before adding the next. Continue until all the stock is absorbed and the rice is tender, about 15–18 minutes. Dot with 2 tablespoons butter, cover and leave to stand for 2 minutes. Meanwhile, heat 1 tablespoon olive oil in a skillet. Cook 4 prosciutto strips for 1 minute on each side until crisp. Remove from the pan and, when cool enough to handle, crumble and set aside. Add 8 cleaned scallops to the same pan and cook for 2 minutes on each side, or until golden. Place the scallops on top of the risotto. Scatter with the crumbled prosciutto and serve.

3⊙ Vietnamese Egg Rolls

Serves 4

vegetable oil, for frying
¼ lb lean ground pork
3½ oz raw peeled small shrimp
scant ½ cup crabmeat
1 garlic clove, crushed
1 teaspoon finely chopped fresh
  ginger root
2 scallions, finely chopped
1 tablespoon soy sauce
pinch of superfine sugar
handful of cilantro, chopped
2 oz dried fine rice noodles
1 tablespoon cornstarch
1 tablespoon water
12 egg roll wrappers
salt and pepper
chili sauce, to serve

- Heat 1 tablespoon oil in a wok or large skillet. Add the pork, shrimp, crabmeat, garlic, ginger, and scallions, and stir-fry for 5 minutes, or until just cooked through. Stir in the soy sauce and sugar and heat until bubbling, then stir in the cilantro and set aside to cool a little. Meanwhile, prepare the noodles according to the package instructions, then drain and add to the seafood mixture.

- Mix the cornstarch with the measurement water. Place a tablespoon of the mixture on one egg roll wrapper. Brush the side with a little of the cornstarch mixture, then fold over and roll up. Repeat with the remaining seafood mixture and wrappers.

- Fill a large saucepan one-third full of oil over medium heat. When a cube of bread dropped in the oil turns brown in 15 seconds the oil is ready. Deep-fry the rolls in batches for 3 minutes, or until golden and crisp. Drain on paper towels. Serve with chili sauce for dipping and an herb salad, if liked.

1⊙ Vietnamese Summer Rolls

Prepare 2 oz dried fine rice noodles according to the package instructions. Drain. Soften 12 rice paper wrappers in very hot water for 30 seconds. Place on damp paper towels. Add some noodles, 2 cooked peeled shrimp, some chopped lettuce, sliced red pepper and carrot, and chopped cilantro to each wrapper. Moisten the edges, fold over and roll up. Serve with chili dipping sauce.

2⊙ Vietnamese Shrimp Skewers

In a food processor, pulse together 10 oz raw peeled shrimp, 1 crushed garlic clove, 2 scallions, 1 teaspoon superfine sugar, 2 teaspoons fish sauce, 1 teaspoon cornstarch, and 1 slice of bacon until smooth. Lightly wet your hands, then shape the mixture around the center of 8 sugar cane sticks or metal skewers. Brush with vegetable oil. Cook on a hot barbecue or smoking hot ridged griddle pan for 5–7 minutes, turning occasionally, until just cooked through. Meanwhile, prepare 10 oz dried fine rice noodles according to the package instructions. Mix together 3 tablespoons fish sauce, 2 teaspoons superfine sugar, and the juice of ½ lime. Drain the noodles. Toss with the sauce and ¼ chopped cucumber. Serve with the skewers.

Seared Tuna with Niçoise Salad

Serves 4

10 oz baby new or salad potatoes, halved

2 eggs

¼ lb green beans

1 tablespoon olive oil

14½ oz very fresh tuna steak

1 cup cherry tomatoes, halved

2 romaine lettuce

8 anchovy fillets in oil, drained

½ cup black olives

salt and pepper

For the vinaigrette

2 garlic cloves, crushed

1 teaspoon Dijon mustard

1 tablespoon red wine vinegar

1 tablespoon lemon juice

¼ cup plus 2 tablespoons extra virgin olive oil

handful of parsley, chopped

- Cook the potatoes in a saucepan of lightly salted boiling water for 12–15 minutes, or until just tender. Drain and cool under cold running water. Meanwhile, gently lower the eggs into a saucepan of boiling water and cook for 8 minutes. Drain and cool as before, then remove the shell. Cook the beans in a saucepan of salted boiling water for 5 minutes until just tender. Drain and cool as before.

- Meanwhile, mix together all the ingredients for the vinaigrette and season well with salt and pepper. Toss half the vinaigrette with the potatoes and beans and set aside. Rub the oil all over the tuna and season well. Heat a ridged griddle pan until smoking hot and cook for 1–2 minutes on each side, or until browned but still rare inside. Cut into bite-size pieces.

- Toss the tomatoes with the potatoes and beans. Separate the leaves of the lettuces, then arrange on a serving plate with the anchovies, olives, eggs, quartered, and the tuna, and drizzle with the remaining dressing.

10 Niçoise Sandwich

Mix together a 3 oz can of tuna in oil, drained, 1 crushed garlic clove, 1 mashed anchovy fillet, and 4 tablespoons mayonnaise. Spread onto 2 slices of bread. Arrange a handful of sun-dried tomatoes, diced, and some arugula leaves on top, then cover each with another slice of bread. Cut in half to serve.

20 Easy Niçoise with Vinaigrette

Cook 2 eggs in boiling water for 8 minutes. Drain and cool under cold running water, then remove the shells. Meanwhile, cook ¼ lb trimmed green beans in lightly salted boiling water for 5 minutes. Drain and cool. Toss the beans with 1 cup cherry tomatoes, 3½ oz chargrilled artichokes from the deli counter or a jar, and ½ cup black olives. Prepare the vinaigrette as above, adding 4 crushed anchovy fillets. Stir a little of this through the bean mixture along with a drained 6 oz can of tuna in oil. Arrange the torn leaves of 2 romaine lettuce on a plate. Place the tuna mixture and quartered eggs on top, and drizzle with the remaining dressing to serve.

Smoked Mackerel Pâté

Serves 4

½ lb smoked mackerel fillets
1 lemon
generous ¾ cup cream cheese
handful of flat-leaf parsley and
   chives, chopped, plus extra
   to serve
salt and pepper
Melba toast, to serve

- Discard the skin and any bones from the fish. Finely grate the zest of about half of the lemon.

- Place the fish and lemon zest in a food processor with the cream cheese and pulse until just combined. Season well with pepper, add salt and the juice from the lemon to taste, and stir in the herbs.

- Place in serving bowls, sprinkle with more herbs, and serve with Melba toast.

 ### Mackerel with Bacon Sauce

Place 1 large gutted mackerel on a lightly greased baking pan. Dot the fish with butter. Place in a preheated oven at 400°F for 15 minutes. Meanwhile, slice 3 slices of bacon into matchsticks and cook in a little olive oil in a saucepan until crisp. Transfer to a plate. To the pan, add 1 diced shallot and cook for 3 minutes. Add 1 crushed garlic clove and cook for 30 seconds. Add ¼ cup dry white wine. Boil until reduced by half. Return the bacon and pour over a generous ¼ cup water. Cook for 2 minutes. Stir in ¼ cup crème fraîche and heat through. Spoon the mixture onto the mackerel, scatter with chopped flat-leaf parsley, and serve.

Creamy Mackerel and Potato Bake

Cook 3 peeled and halved potatoes in a saucepan of lightly salted boiling water for 10–15 minutes, or until just cooked through. Drain, then slice as thinly as you can. Meanwhile, heat 2 tablespoons butter in a saucepan. Add 1 diced onion and cook for 5 minutes until softened. Stir in a scant ½ cup heavy cream. Discard the skin and any bones from 2 x 5 oz smoked mackerel fillets, then break into flakes. Stir through the sauce along with 1 teaspoon wholegrain mustard. Mix with the potato slices and place in a lightly greased baking dish. Scatter with ½ cup dried bread crumbs and drizzle with olive oil. Cook under a preheated hot broiler for 5–10 minutes, or until bubbling and golden. Serve immediately with a green salad.

FIS-LIGH-SYL

Chinese Crab and Sweetcorn Soup

Serves 4

3 cobs of corn
5 cups chicken stock
1 tablespoon Shaoxing wine
1 tablespoon soy sauce
2 teaspoons minced fresh ginger root
2 teaspoons cornstarch
1 tablespoon water
1½ cups white crabmeat
1 egg, beaten
2 scallions, diced
salt and pepper

- Use a sharp knife to cut the kernels from the cobs of corn. Place both the kernels and the cobs in a large saucepan with the stock and simmer for 12 minutes. Remove and discard the cobs. Scoop out half the kernels and set aside. Puree the remainder with a stick blender until creamy.

- Return the whole kernels to the pan along with the Shaoxing wine, soy sauce, and ginger. Mix the cornstarch with the measurement water and stir into the soup along with the crabmeat. Simmer until heated through and slightly thickened. Season with salt and pepper to taste.

- Stirring the soup with a large spoon, slowly pour in the egg in one long stream to create silky strands of egg through the soup. Scatter with the scallions and serve.

 Crab and Sweetcorn Bites

Mix together a 6 oz can of white crabmeat, drained, ½ cup whole kernel sweet corn, 1 sliced scallion, 1 tablespoon self-rising flour, and 1 beaten egg. Heat 1 tablespoon vegetable oil in a nonstick skillet and drop large spoonfuls of the mixture separately into the pan. Cook for 2–3 minutes on each side, or until golden and serve.

 Sweetcorn Risotto with Crab

Heat 1 tablespoon olive oil and 1 tablespoon butter in a large saucepan. Cook 1 diced onion for 5 minutes until softened. Stir in 1½ cups risotto rice until well coated. Pour in ¼ cup dry white wine and cook until nearly boiled off. Add about 4¼ cups vegetable stock, a ladleful at a time, stirring and simmering after each addition until the stock is absorbed before adding the next ladleful. Meanwhile, cook ½ cup whole kernel sweet corn in boiling water for 5 minutes until soft. Drain, then pulse in a food processor with 5 tablespoons crème fraîche until smooth. After 15 minutes of cooking the risotto (when all the stock is absorbed and the rice is nearly cooked through), add the pureed sweetcorn and cook for a few minutes more until the rice is tender. Stir in a drained 6 oz can of white crabmeat. Place spoonfuls of crème fraîche on top and scatter with chopped chives to serve.

30 Baked Eggs with Smoked Fish and Leeks

Serves 4

¾ cup milk
8 oz smoked haddock fillet
2 tablespoons butter
2 small leeks, thinly sliced
1 tablespoon all-purpose flour
3 tablespoons crème fraîche
4 eggs
salt and pepper
toasted brown bread, to serve

- Pour the milk over the haddock in a shallow saucepan. Simmer over low heat for 7–10 minutes, or until the fish flakes easily. Pour the milk through a strainer into a jug. When the fish is cool enough to handle, tear into flakes, discarding the skin and any bones.

- Meanwhile, melt half the butter in a saucepan. Add the leeks and a splash of water and cook for 5 minutes, or until soft. Stir in the flour and cook for 2 minutes. Slowly whisk in the poaching milk until smooth. Bring to a boil, whisking, then simmer for a few minutes, or until slightly thickened. Season well with salt and pepper. Stir in the crème fraîche.

- Divide the leek mixture between 4 individual ramekins or ovenproof dishes on a cookie sheet. Arrange the haddock on top. Crack an egg into each and dot with the remaining butter. Place in a preheated oven at 350°F and cook for 10–12 minutes, or until the white is set and the yolks are still soft. Serve with toasted brown bread.

 Creamy Smoked Fish Scrambled Eggs Crack 5 eggs into a nonstick saucepan over medium heat. Scatter small spoonfuls of ¼ cup crème fraîche all over the surface and leave for 1–2 minutes. Stir once, then leave for 30 seconds more. Shred a 4 oz skinless smoked mackerel fillet into small flakes using a fork. Discard any bones. Gently stir into the eggs. When the eggs are just setting but still creamy and moist, scatter with some chopped chives and serve on toast.

 Puffed Smoked Fish Omelet Pour ¾ cup milk over an 8 oz smoked haddock fillet in a shallow pan. Simmer over low heat for 7–10 minutes, or until cooked through. Drain. When the fish is cool enough to handle, shred into flakes using a fork. Discard the skin and any bones. Meanwhile, separate 4 eggs. Lightly mix together the egg yolks with plenty of seasoning. Carefully whisk the egg whites in a grease-free bowl until just stiff. Stir one-third of the whites into the yolks, then carefully add the remainder in 2 batches. Heat 1 tablespoon butter in a nonstick skillet. Add the egg mixture and cook for 1 minute then scatter the shredded smoked haddock on top. Place the pan under a preheated medium broiler, making sure you turn the handle away from the heat if not flameproof, and cook for a further 5 minutes, or until puffed and just set. Scatter with 1 chopped scallion and serve immediately.

 Anchovy and Olive Crostini

Serves 4

½ baguette, thickly sliced on an angle
1 large garlic clove, peeled
4 tablespoons extra virgin olive oil
3 tomatoes, diced
4 anchovy fillets in oil, drained and sliced
1 teaspoon drained capers
½ cup pitted black olives, roughly chopped
handful of basil, chopped
salt and pepper

- Place the baguette slices on a large broiler pan. Toast under a preheated hot broiler for 3 minutes. Turn the slices over and toast the other side until golden and crisp.

- Rub a little of the garlic clove over each piece of toasted bread, then drizzle with 2 tablespoons of the oil.

- Mix together the remaining ingredients and season well with salt and pepper. Spoon a little of the mixture onto each slice of toasted bread and serve.

Bread, Anchovy, and Olive Salad

Cut ½ baguette into bite-size pieces. Arrange on a baking pan and place in a preheated oven at 400°F for 12 minutes, or until just golden and crisp. Meanwhile, mash together 3 drained anchovy fillets in oil and 1 crushed garlic clove until smooth. Whisk in 5 tablespoons extra virgin olive oil, 1 tablespoon red wine, and a good pinch of dried red pepper flakes. Toss together the bread and 5 diced tomatoes, then drizzle with the anchovy dressing. Leave for 5 minutes, then stir through ½ cup pitted black olives and a handful of arugula to serve.

Onion, Anchovy, and Olive Puffs

Heat 2 tablespoons olive oil in a skillet over low heat. Add 2 thinly sliced large onions and gently cook for 10 minutes, or until soft and golden. Meanwhile, use a 3 inch round cookie cutter to cut out 4 rounds from a 12 oz sheet of puff pastry. Set the rounds on a cookie sheet. Spread 2 tablespoons ready-made tomato pasta sauce onto each round, then spoon the cooked onions evenly onto the sauce. Arrange 2 drained anchovy fillets in oil on top of each round and scatter with ½ cup pitted black olives. Place in a preheated oven at 400°F for 15 minutes, or until crisp and cooked through.

Broiled Lemony Oysters with Spinach

Serves 4

1 tablespoon olive oil

¼ lb spinach, washed

scant ½ cup butter

2 egg yolks

lemon juice, to taste

1 teaspoon Worcestershire sauce

pinch of cayenne

12 live oysters, opened but in the shell

salt and pepper

- Heat the oil in a large saucepan over medium heat. Add the spinach and a splash of water and cook for 2 minutes, or until wilted. Drain, pressing out the liquid, and finely chop.

- Melt the butter in a small saucepan until bubbling but not brown. Set a small heatproof bowl over a saucepan of simmering water, ensuring that the bottom of the bowl doesn't touch the water. Add the egg yolks and a good squeeze of lemon juice and whisk together. Whisking continuously, very slowly start to add the melted butter. As the mixture starts to thicken, you can add the butter a little more quickly. When thickened, season with salt and pepper, and add more lemon juice to taste, the Worcestershire sauce, and cayenne.

- Discard the top shell of each oyster. Place a little spinach onto each oyster and dust with more cayenne. Set them in a broiler pan and spoon some sauce into each. Cook under a hot broiler for 1 minute, or until the sauce is lightly browned.

 Smoked Mussel and Spinach Pasta

Cook 13 oz fresh fettuccine according to the package instructions. When the pasta is just cooked, stir in ¼ lb washed spinach, then drain immediately, reserving some of the cooking water, and return to the pan. Meanwhile, mix together 3½ oz smoked mussels, 1 beaten egg, and 1–2 teaspoons fresh lemon juice. Stir the mussel mixture through the pasta, adding a little of the reserved cooking water to loosen if necessary, then serve.

 Oyster and Spinach Open Sandwich

Split 2 individual baguettes in half lengthwise. Wrap in foil, then place in a preheated oven at 400°F for 15 minutes, or until crisp. Leave to cool for 5 minutes. Meanwhile, beat 1 egg. Mix in 12 shucked live oysters. Toss ¾ cup polenta with ½ teaspoon cayenne. Allow any excess egg to drip away from the oysters, then toss them in the spiced polenta until coated. Fill a large, deep saucepan over medium-high heat one-third full with vegetable oil. When a cube of bread dropped into the oil turns brown in 15 seconds the oil is ready. Deep-fry the oysters in batches for 2–3 minutes, or until crisp and golden. Drain on paper towels. While the oysters are frying, roughly chop 3 cups mixed spinach, arugula, and watercress. Mix a good squeeze of lemon juice into ¼ cup mayonnaise and spread on the baked baguette halves. Place the salad on top, then add the warm fried oysters to serve.

30 Charred Tomato, Shrimp, and Feta Salad

Serves 4

1¼ cups cherry tomatoes, halved

5 tablespoons olive oil, plus extra for oiling

handful of oregano leaves, chopped

1 teaspoon crushed fennel seeds

5 oz cooked peeled jumbo shrimp, tails on

1 tablespoon balsamic vinegar

4 cups arugula

½ cup crumbled feta cheese

salt and pepper

- Place the tomatoes on a lightly oiled baking pan. Drizzle with the oil, season with salt and pepper, then scatter a little of the oregano and crushed fennel seeds onto each tomato. Place in a preheated oven at 400°F and cook for 15–20 minutes until browned and slightly shriveled. Leave to cool for a few minutes.

- Toss the juices from the baking pan with the balsamic vinegar and shrimp. Then arrange on a serving plate with the arugula and cooked tomatoes. Scatter with the crumbled feta to serve.

---

10 Shrimp with Sun-Dried Tomato

Feta Dip Mash together a generous ¼ cup cream cheese and 1 oz feta cheese until smooth, then thin the mixture with a little milk. Stir in 3 diced sun-dried tomatoes and a handful of basil, chopped. Arrange 7 oz cooked jumbo peeled shrimp on a plate and serve with the dip.

---

20 Shrimp Pasta with Tomatoes and Feta

Place 1¼ cups halved cherry tomatoes on a lightly oiled baking pan. Drizzle with 5 tablespoons olive oil, then scatter with a handful of oregano leaves, chopped, and 1 teaspoon crushed fennel seeds. Place in a preheated oven at 400°F for 15–18 minutes until browned and slightly shriveled. Meanwhile, cook 11 oz dried trofie pasta according to the package instructions.

Add ¼ lb raw peeled jumbo shrimp for the last 3 minutes of cooking and cook until they turn pink. Drain, reserving some of the cooking water, and return to the pan. Crumble 2 oz feta cheese and scatter it into the pasta with a little of the reserved cooking water. Stir until you have a smooth sauce. Stir in the cooked tomatoes and then spoon into serving bowls. Chop 1 cup arugula, scatter onto the pasta, and serve.

Smoked Trout Pasta with Creamy Dill Sauce

Serves 4

13 oz fresh linguine
6 tablespoons crème fraîche
squeeze of lemon juice
handful of dill, finely chopped,
  plus extra to serve
2 skinless smoked trout fillets,
  weighing about 4 oz each
2 scallions, diced
salt and pepper

- Cook the linguine according to the package instructions.

- Meanwhile, mix together the crème fraîche, lemon juice, and dill to make a smooth sauce. Break the trout into bite-size pieces.

- Drain the pasta, reserving a little of the cooking water. Return to the pan and stir through the sauce, trout, and scallions. Season well with salt and pepper, and add a little of the reserved cooking water to loosen. Serve immediately, scattered with extra dill.

Potato Rösti with Smoked Trout

Cook 2 peeled large round red or round white potatoes in a saucepan of boiling water for 5 minutes. Cool under the cold running water and pat dry. Roughly grate then add 1–2 teaspoons fresh lemon juice to prevent discoloration. Using your hands, squeeze out any excess liquid. Form into small patties and dust each with flour. Heat 1 tablespoon each of olive oil and butter in a nonstick skillet. Add the patties and cook for 3–5 minutes on each side, or until golden and cooked through. Spoon 1 teaspoon crème fraîche onto each, add a large flake of smoked trout, and scatter with finely chopped dill to serve.

Smoked Trout Eggs

Cook 4 eggs in a saucepan of boiling water for 6 minutes. Drain and cool under cold running water, then remove the shells. In a food processor, pulse together 7 oz each skinless smoked trout fillets and skinless fresh salmon fillet, the finely grated zest of 1 lemon, and a handful of dill, chopped, until you have a smooth paste. Lightly wet your hands, then divide the paste into 4 and wrap a layer around each egg so that it is entirely encased. Dip the encased eggs into 1 beaten egg, then roll in 1 cup dried bread crumbs to coat. Fill a large, deep saucepan one-third full with vegetable oil over medium heat.

When a cube of bread dropped in the oil turns brown in 20 seconds the oil is ready. Deep-fry the eggs, in batches if necessary to avoid overcrowding the pan and causing the oil temperature to drop, for 3–4 minutes until golden and crisp all over. Drain on paper towels and serve with lemon wedges.

Salt and Pepper Squid Bites

Serves 4–6

1 lb cleaned squid

2 teaspoons peppercorns, crushed

1 teaspoon dried red pepper flakes

2 teaspoons salt

¾ cup all-purpose flour

vegetable oil, for deep-frying

2 scallions, cut into thick slices

1 red chile, cut into thick strips

lemon wedges, to serve

- Cut each squid tube in half. Lay flat, inside facing up, and use a sharp knife to gently score a cross. Cut into bite-size pieces, then pat dry with paper towels.

- Mix together the crushed peppercorns, dried red pepper flakes, salt, and flour. Toss the squid in the mixture.

- Fill a large, deep saucepan one-third full with oil over medium heat. When a cube of bread dropped in the oil turns brown in 15 seconds the oil is ready. Shake off the excess flour from a handful of squid and deep-fry for 2–3 minutes, or until just golden and crisp. Drain on paper towels. Keep warm in the oven. Repeat with the remaining squid.

- Deep-fry the scallions and chile strips for 1–2 minutes, and use to garnish the squid. Serve with lemon wedges.

Stir-Fried Salt and Pepper Squid

Crush together 1 teaspoon salt, ½ teaspoon pepper, and a pinch each of Chinese five-spice powder and dried red pepper flakes. Cut 1 lb cleaned squid into thick rings. Heat 1 tablespoon vegetable oil in a wok and stir-fry half the squid for 1 minute. Remove from the wok, add another tablespoon of oil, and stir-fry the remaining squid for 1 minute. Return the first batch of squid to the wok along with the salt mix and 1 sliced scallion. Stir around in the wok until the squid is well coated, then serve immediately.

 Salt and Pepper Squid Bites with Chili Jam For the chili jam, place 2 large tomatoes in a saucepan with 1 cup superfine sugar and 4 minced red chiles. Add ¼ cup apple cider vinegar, 1 tablespoon fish sauce, and 1–2 teaspoons fresh lime juice. Bring to a boil and let the mixture bubble until the sugar dissolves. Then simmer for 20 minutes until sticky and thickened. Meanwhile, prepare and deep-fry the squid as above. Serve hot with the chili jam.

 # Moroccan Sardine Pita Breads

Serves 4

2 sardines, weighing about
3½ oz each, boned and each
cut into 2 fillets
1 teaspoon ground cumin
pinch of cayenne
pinch of all-purpose flour
3 tablespoons olive oil
1 tablespoon finely chopped
preserved lemon
handful of cilantro, chopped
handful of flat-leaf parsley,
chopped
4 pita breads
1 tomato, chopped
¼ cucumber, sliced
salt and pepper

- Pat the sardines dry with paper towels and season with salt and pepper. Mix together the cumin, cayenne, and flour. Dust the fish all over with the spice mixture.

- Heat 1 tablespoon of the oil in a large, nonstick skillet. Cook the fish, skin-side down, for 5 minutes. Turn over and fry for a further 3 minutes until cooked through. Keep warm.

- Mix the remaining oil with the preserved lemon and herbs, then season well. Lightly toast the pita breads.

- Fill the pita breads with the fish, tomato, and cucumber, then drizzle over the dressing to serve.

 ### Deviled Sardines on Toast

Toast 4 thick slices of country bread. Heat 2 x 3¾ oz cans of sardines in tomato sauce with ½ teaspoon ground cumin and a pinch of cayenne until warmed through. Spoon over the toast and scatter with 1 tablespoon each diced onion and chopped flat-leaf parsley to serve.

 ### Spiced Moroccan Sardine Curry

Heat 2 tablespoons olive oil in a large, deep skillet. Cook 1 diced onion for 5 minutes. Stir in 2 minced garlic cloves and cook for 2 minutes. Add 1 teaspoon each ground cumin and ground coriander followed by 2 teaspoons tomato paste. Stir in a 13½ oz can diced tomatoes and a little water. Leave to simmer for 10 minutes. Meanwhile, in a food processor, pulse together 1 lb skinless sardine fillets, 1 egg yolk, 1 teaspoon paprika, the finely grated zest of 1 lemon, and a handful each of parsley and cilantro until smooth. Lightly wet your hands, then roll into walnut-sized balls. Season, then carefully add the fishballs to the pan. Simmer for 7–10 minutes, or until cooked through. Scatter with some more herbs, if you like, and serve with steamed couscous.

Steamed Mussels in Wine

Serves 4

2 tablespoons olive oil
2 garlic cloves, sliced
3 lb cleaned live mussels
1 scant cup dry white wine
handful of flat-leaf parsley,
  chopped
crusty bread, to serve

- Heat the oil in a large saucepan. Add the garlic and cook for 30 seconds until lightly golden. Add the mussels and wine.

- Cover the pan and cook for 5 minutes, shaking the pan occasionally, until the mussels have opened. Discard any that remain closed.

- Stir in the parsley, then serve with crusty bread.

 ### Mussel and Bacon Pasta

Heat 2 tablespoons olive oil in a saucepan. Cut 2 slices of bacon into matchsticks and cook for 3–5 minutes, or until golden. Add 1 minced shallot and cook for 3 minutes. Stir in 2 sliced garlic cloves, 1½ lb cleaned live mussels, and 1 scant cup dry white wine. Cover and cook for 5–7 minutes, or until the mussels have opened. Discard any that remain closed. Meanwhile, cook 11 oz dried spaghetti according to the package instructions. Drain the pasta and return to the pan. Lift out the mussels and add to the pasta. Boil to reduce the mussel liquid, if necessary, then stir in ¼ cup crème fraîche. Toss with the pasta. Scatter with chopped flat-leaf parsley and serve.

Crispy Baked Mussels

Heat 2 tablespoons olive oil in a large saucepan. Cook 2 sliced garlic cloves for 30 seconds until lightly golden. Add 3 lb cleaned live mussels and 1 scant cup dry white wine, then season with salt. Cover and cook for 4 minutes until the mussels are just starting to open. Strain, reserving the liquid. Leave to cool a little, then discard any mussels that remain closed. Discard one half-shell from each mussel, leaving the mussels inside the remaining half-shells. Arrange on a baking pan. Boil the reserved liquid until reduced to ¼ cup. Stir in a scant ½ cup heavy cream and boil until reduced to a generous ¼ cup then stir through a handful of chopped flat-leaf parsley. Spoon a little of the sauce onto each mussel in its half-shell. Carefully scatter some dried bread crumbs onto each mussel and put a small pat of butter on top. Place in a preheated oven at 425°F for 5 minutes, or until golden and bubbling.

Corn Cakes with Smoked Salmon

Serves 4

2 eggs, beaten
4 tablespoons milk
8½ oz can whole kernel sweet corn, drained
generous ¼ cup self-rising flour
2 scallions, sliced
2 tablespoons vegetable oil
5 oz smoked salmon
¼ cup mascarpone cheese
salt and pepper
chopped chives, to garnish

- Beat together the eggs, milk, whole kernel sweet corn, flour, and scallions until you have a smooth batter. Season well with salt and pepper.

- Heat 1 tablespoon of the oil in a large, nonstick skillet. Add half the batter to the pan in separate spoonfuls to make 6 small pancakes. Cook for 2–3 minutes on each side, or until golden and cooked through. Set aside on paper towels while you cook the remaining batter.

- Pile the pancakes onto serving plates and arrange the smoked salmon and mascarpone on top. Scatter with the chives and serve.

Simple Corn and Salmon Pasta

Cook 13 oz fresh penne according to the package instructions. Add scant ¾ cup frozen corn kernels for the last minute of cooking. Drain and return to the pan. Stir in 5 tablespoons crème fraîche and 5 oz smoked salmon, torn into strips. Scatter with a handful of chopped chives to serve.

Cajun Salmon with Corn Salsa

Make a Cajun spice mix by stirring together 1 tablespoon salt, 2 teaspoons paprika, 1 teaspoon ground cumin, ½ teaspoon each dried oregano and basil and a good pinch each of cayenne and pepper. Set aside half for another time and mix the remainder with 1 crushed garlic clove and 2 tablespoons olive oil. Rub all over 4 x 6 oz salmon steaks and leave to marinate for 10–15 minutes. Cook on a hot barbecue or a smoking hot ridged griddle pan for 5–7 minutes on each side until charred and cooked through. Meanwhile, use a sharp knife to cut the kernels from 2 cobs of corn. Heat 1 tablespoon vegetable oil in a skillet and cook until golden. Leave to cool a little, then stir through 1 chopped tomato, a squeeze of lime juice, and some chopped cilantro before serving.

Kipper Salad with Creamy Mustard Dressing

Serves 4

¾ lb baby new or salad potatoes, halved
2 skinless kipper fillets, weighing about 7½ oz each
oil, for brushing
3½ cups watercress
salt and pepper

For the dressing

generous ¼ cup sour cream
1 teaspoon wholegrain mustard
pinch of superfine sugar
1 tablespoon diced red onion

- Cook the potatoes in a saucepan of lightly salted boiling water for 12–15 minutes, or until just tender. Drain and cool under cold running water, then drain again.

- Meanwhile, lightly brush the kipper fillets with oil and place under a preheated hot broiler for 7–10 minutes, or until cooked through. Remove from the broiler and flake the flesh, discarding any skin and bones.

- Mix together the sour cream, mustard, and sugar, then season with salt and pepper.

- Arrange the potatoes, watercress, and fish on serving plates. Scatter with the onion, pour on the dressing, and serve.

Rollmops with Mustard Dressing

Arrange 8 rollmops or cured herring fillets on a plate along with 1 chopped ready-cooked fresh beet. Mix together 5 tablespoons sour cream, 1 teaspoon wholegrain mustard, a pinch of superfine sugar, and a handful of dill, chopped. Drizzle the dressing over the fish and beets, and serve with slices of crusty bread.

Herring with Mustard Sauce

Heat 1 tablespoon olive oil in a skillet over medium heat. Add 1 sliced onion and cook for about 10 minutes, or until very soft. Transfer to a shallow baking dish and arrange 4 x 8 oz herrings, gutted and scaled, on top. Meanwhile, melt 2 tablespoons butter in a saucepan, stir in 2 tablespoons all-purpose flour, and cook for 2 minutes. Slowly whisk in 1¼ cups milk until smooth. Bring to a boil, whisking continuously, then simmer for a few minutes until thickened. Stir in ¼ cup crème fraîche, 2 teaspoons wholegrain mustard, and some chopped dill and then pour the mixture onto the fish. Place in a preheated oven at 375°F for 15 minutes, or until the fish is just cooked through.

Crayfish Cocktail

Serves 4

generous ¼ cup mayonnaise
2 tablespoons tomato ketchup
Tabasco sauce, to taste
lemon juice, to taste
10 oz cooked peeled crayfish tails
2 Little Gem lettuces, leaves
  separated
2 small ripe avocado, stoned,
  peeled, and sliced
salt and pepper
paprika, to garnish

- Mix together the mayonnaise and ketchup, add the Tabasco and lemon juice to taste and season with salt and pepper. Stir the mixture through the crayfish.

- Pile the lettuce leaves into serving bowls and add the avocado. Spoon the crayfish mixture on top. Dust with paprika to garnish and serve immediately.

Mexican-Style Seafood Cocktail

Place 5 oz raw peeled shrimp in a bowl. Add boiling water to cover and leave for 2 minutes. Add 5 oz cleaned scallops, pouring in a little more boiling water, and leave for a further 3 minutes, then drain. Mix together 1¼ cups tomato juice, 1 tablespoon tomato ketchup, 1–2 teaspoons fresh lime juice, and a dash of Tabasco sauce to taste. Stir into the seafood and leave to stand for 10 minutes. Divide the mixture among serving bowls. Place a chopped avocado, 1 sliced scallion, and a handful of chopped cilantro on top to serve.

Shrimp in Warm Cocktail Sauce

Melt a scant ½ cup butter in a small saucepan until bubbling but not brown. Set a small heatproof bowl over a saucepan of simmering water, ensuring that the bottom of the bowl doesn't touch the water. Add 2 egg yolks and 1–2 teaspoons fresh lemon juice and whisk together. Whisking constantly, very slowly start to add the melted butter. As the mixture starts to thicken, you can add the remainder a little more quickly. When thickened, leave to cool a little, then stir in 2 teaspoons tomato paste and a handful of chopped tarragon.

In a separate bowl, whisk a scant ½ cup whipping cream until soft peaks form. Stir this into the sauce, season, and add Tabasco to taste. Stir in ¾ lb cooked peeled jumbo shrimp and spoon into individual gratin dishes. Place under a preheated hot broiler and cook for 3 minutes, or until lightly browned.

Indian Shrimp Omelet Wraps

Serves 4

3 tablespoons vegetable oil

1 onion, sliced

2 garlic cloves, crushed

1 teaspoon minced fresh ginger root

½ teaspoon ground cumin

7 oz small raw peeled shrimp

2 tomatoes, diced

4 eggs, beaten

1 teaspoon garam masala

1 green chile, minced

handful of cilantro, chopped

salt and pepper

4 warmed chapatis, to serve

- Heat 1 tablespoon of the oil in a skillet over medium heat. Add the onion and cook for 5 minutes, or until softened, then add the garlic, ginger, and cumin and cook for a further minute. Stir in the shrimp and cook for 3 minutes. Add the tomatoes and continue to cook until the shrimp are pink and cooked through.

- Mix together the eggs, garam masala, and chile and season well with salt and pepper. Heat ½ tablespoon of the remaining oil in a small, nonstick skillet. Add one-quarter of the egg mixture and swirl around the pan. Stir once, then leave to cook for 1–2 minutes, or until starting to set. Spoon one-quarter of the tomato shrimp mixture on top and scatter with a little chopped cilantro. Place on a warmed chapati and fold in half. Repeat with the remaining ingredients.

Spicy Scrambled Eggs with Shrimp

Mix together 1 teaspoon curry paste and 3 tablespoons crème fraîche. Crack 4 eggs into a nonstick saucepan and scatter with teaspoonsful of the crème fraîche mixture. Season and cook over a low heat for 3 minutes. When the mixture starts to set, add 2 oz cooked peeled small shrimp and cook, stirring occasionally and breaking up the egg yolks, until creamy and just cooked through. Scatter with a handful of chopped cilantro and serve immediately.

Indonesian Shrimp and Egg Curry

Heat 1 tablespoon vegetable oil in a saucepan. Add 1 diced onion, 3 crushed garlic cloves, and 2 teaspoons minced fresh ginger root or galangal. Cook for 5 minutes, or until softened. Stir in 1 tablespoon rendang or Thai red curry paste and ½ teaspoon turmeric. Cook for 1 minute. Pour in 1 scant cup chicken stock and 1 cup coconut milk. Add 2 lemon grass stalks and 2 fresh lime leaves. Leave to simmer for 10–15 minutes. Meanwhile, cook 4 eggs in a saucepan of boiling water for 8 minutes. Drain and cool under cold running water, then remove the shells. Stir 7 oz raw peeled jumbo shrimp and the eggs into the curry. Simmer for 5 minutes, or until the shrimp are pink or just cooked through. Scatter with chopped cilantro and serve.

10 Tuscan Tuna and Bean Salad

Serves 4

5 tablespoons mayonnaise
6 oz can tuna in oil, drained
¾ cup canned cannellini beans,
   rinsed and drained
1 lemon
2½ cups arugula
½ small red onion, diced
1 tablespoon olive oil
salt and pepper

- Carefully mix the mayonnaise with the tuna and beans, being careful not to break the tuna up too much.

- Finely grate about half the zest of the lemon. Toss the arugula and onion with the lemon zest. Whisk together the oil and a good squeeze of juice from the lemon, then season with salt and pepper.

- Toss the arugula salad with the dressing, arrange in serving bowls, and place the tuna and beans on top to serve.

---

2 Tuna with Mashed Beans

Cook 1 diced small onion in 1 tablespoon butter in a saucepan for 5 minutes. Add 1 crushed garlic clove. Cook for 1 minute. Add a scant ½ cup light cream and a scant ½ cup stock. Bring to a boil. Add 2 x 15 oz cans cannellini beans, rinsed and drained, and 1 thyme sprig. Simmer for 10 minutes. Discard the thyme and mash the beans to a smooth paste. Meanwhile, brush 1 tablespoon olive oil over 4 x 5 oz tuna steaks. Cook on a smoking hot ridged griddle pan for 3 minutes on each side. Season everything well and serve with the beans.

3 Tuna and Bean Pasta Bake

Cook 11 oz dried penne according to the package instructions. Add ¾ cup rinsed and drained canned cannellini beans for the last 2 minutes of cooking. Drain the pasta and beans and return them to the pan. Meanwhile, melt 3 tablespoons butter in a saucepan, stir in a generous ¼ cup all-purpose flour, and cook for 2 minutes. Slowly whisk in 2 cups milk until smooth. Bring to a boil, whisking, then simmer for a few minutes until thickened. Stir into the pasta and beans along with a drained 6 oz can of tuna in oil. Transfer to a baking dish. Combine ½ cup dried bread crumbs with the finely grated zest of 1 lemon and scatter the mixture evenly over everything. Place the dish in a preheated oven at 400°F for 15 minutes until crisp and browned on top.

30 Seafood Risotto

Serves 6

8 oz mixed fish fillets, such as sea
  bass, monkfish and striped
  mullet, cut into 1 inch chunks
7 oz raw small shrimp, shells on
3¼ pints fish stock
¾ cup dry white wine
1 tablespoon olive oil
2 tablespoons butter
1 small onion, diced
½ fennel bulb, diced
1 lb risotto rice
8 oz cleaned live clams
3½ oz raw squid rings
fresh lemon juice, to taste
salt and pepper

- Place the fish and shrimp in a large saucepan. Pour in the stock and wine and bring to a boil. Cook for 1–2 minutes, or until the seafood just turns opaque. Remove from the pan and set aside. Keep the stock simmering.

- Heat the oil with a little of the butter in a large saucepan. Add the onion and fennel and cook for 5 minutes. Stir in the rice until well coated. Add the hot stock, a ladleful at a time, stirring and simmering after each addition until the stock is absorbed before adding the next. After 15 minutes, when the stock is absorbed and the rice is nearly cooked through, add the clams and cook for 3 minutes, then add the cooked seafood, squid rings, and remaining butter. Season with salt and pepper and add lemon juice to taste.

- Cover and leave to stand for 2 minutes. Pick out and discard any clams that remain closed and serve.

 Seafood Noodle Broth

Heat 3¼ pints (6¼ cups) stock, 2 slices fresh ginger root, and 1 lemon grass stalk in a large saucepan. Add 8 oz cleaned live clams, 3½ oz raw peeled shrimp, and 7 oz dried fine rice noodles. Cook for 3 minutes. Add 3 oz raw squid rings. Boil for 2 minutes, or until all the seafood is cooked. Discard any clams that remain closed. Scatter with chopped cilantro to serve.

 Seafood Rice

Cook 1 lb white long-grain rice in a large saucepan of salted boiling water for 15 minutes, or until tender. Add 1¼ cups frozen peas and 3½ oz frozen raw squid rings for the final 3 minutes of cooking. Drain and return to the pan. Shred 4 x 4 oz skinless smoked mackerel fillets into large flakes, discarding any bones. Stir the flakes through the rice along with 3 thinly sliced scallions and 2–3 teaspoons fresh lemon juice. Scatter with plenty of chopped flat-leaf parsley to serve.

Mackerel Goujons with Sour Cream and Paprika Dip

Serves 4

2 mackerel fillets, weighing about 6 oz each, cut into strips

generous ½ cup all-purpose flour

1 egg, beaten

¾ cup dried bread crumbs

2 garlic cloves, crushed

vegetable oil, for deep-frying

2 teaspoons smoked paprika

¼ cup plus 2 tablespoons sour cream

salt and pepper

- Pat the fish dry with paper towels. Roll in the flour to coat then dip into the beaten egg. Mix together the bread crumbs and garlic, then season well with salt and pepper. Press the fish gently into the bread crumb mixture until well coated.

- Fill a large, deep saucepan one-third full with vegetable oil over medium heat. When a cube of bread dropped in the oil turns brown in 15 seconds the oil is ready. Deep-fry the fish in batches for about 3 minutes, or until golden, crisp, and cooked through. Drain on paper towels.

- Mix most of the paprika into the sour cream saving a pinch of paprika to dust on top. Place the dip in a small bowl and serve with the hot goujons.

 Simple Broiled Paprika Mackerel

Drizzle 2 tablespoons olive oil all over 4 x 6 oz mackerel fillets and season. Cook, skin-side up, under a hot broiler for 5 minutes. Turn over and cook for a further 3 minutes, or until just cooked through. Scatter with 2 minced garlic cloves, 2 teaspoons smoked paprika, and a small handful chopped flat-leaf parsley. Serve with lemon wedges on the side.

 Mackerel with Paprika Onion

Crust Heat 2 tablespoons olive oil in a skillet over medium heat. Add 1 sliced onion and cook for 10 minutes, or until soft. Stir in 2 minced garlic cloves and cook for a further 2 minutes. Place 2 x 6 oz mackerel fillets on a baking pan and place the onion and garlic mixture on top of them. Combine ½ cup dried bread crumbs, 1 tablespoon smoked paprika, the finely grated zest of 1 lemon, and a handful of chopped parsley and scatter the mixture onto the fish. Drizzle with a little more olive oil. Place in a preheated oven at 400°F for 15 minutes, or until crisp and the fish is cooked through.

 # Garlicky Shrimp and Sherry Tapas

Serves 4

10 oz raw jumbo shrimp, tails on
2 tablespoons olive oil
2 garlic cloves, sliced
3 tablespoons fino or other
   dry sherry
salt
handful of flat-leaf parsley,
   chopped, to garnish

- Heat the oil in a skillet over medium heat. Add the garlic followed a few seconds later by the shrimp. Cook for 3 minutes, turning once, until golden. Pour in the sherry and let it bubble for 1–2 minutes. Season with salt, scatter with the parsley, and serve immediately.

 ## Spanish Shrimp and Sherry Stew

Heat 2 tablespoons olive oil in a saucepan over medium heat and add 3 sliced garlic cloves. Cook for 30 seconds until golden. Add a 13½ oz can diced tomatoes, 3 tablespoons dry sherry, and ½ teaspoon smoked paprika. Cook for 15 minutes. Meanwhile, cook 1 lb baby new or salad potatoes in a saucepan of lightly salted boiling water for 12 minutes, or until tender. Drain and add to the stew along with ½ lb raw peeled jumbo shrimp. Cook for a further 3–5 minutes, or until the shrimp are cooked, then stir in 3 tablespoons crème fraîche. Serve with crusty bread.

 ## Shrimp and Sherry Dim Sum

In a food processor, pulse together ½ lb raw peeled shrimp, 1 tablespoon dry sherry, 1 teaspoon sesame oil, ½ teaspoon minced fresh ginger root, 1 crushed garlic clove, and a pinch of superfine sugar until smooth. Stir in 2 diced scallions. Place 16 round won ton wrappers on a cutting board and place a heaped teaspoon of the mixture on one half of each wrapper. Lightly wet your hands, then use your fingers to moisten the edge of each wrapper. Fold each wrapper over to form a half-moon shape, pressing with your thumb and forefinger to make little pleats and entirely enclosing the filling. Heat 2 tablespoons vegetable oil in a nonstick skillet. Fry the dumplings for 2–3 minutes until golden. Pour ¼ cup vegetable stock into the skillet with the dumplings, cover, and simmer/steam for 5–7 minutes, or until cooked through. Serve with soy sauce for dipping.

 # Best Crab Sandwich Ever

Serves 2

3 tablespoons brown crabmeat
2 tablespoons mayonnaise
pinch of cayenne
1 teaspoon tomato ketchup
fresh lemon juice, to taste
4 slices of crusty brown bread
generous ½ cup white crabmeat
salt and pepper
1 cup watercress
lightly salted potato chips, to
    serve (optional)

- Mix together the brown crabmeat, mayonnaise, cayenne, and ketchup. Add lemon juice to taste and season with salt and pepper.

- Spread the crab mixture over 2 slices of the bread then scatter with the white crabmeat and watercress. Place the remaining slices of bread on top. Cut diagonally in half and serve with some lightly salted potato chips, if you like.

 Melting Crab Toasts

Mix together 2 sliced scallions, 2¼ cups white crabmeat, and a generous ¼ cup crème fraîche. Add 2–3 teaspoons fresh lemon juice and a splash of Tabasco sauce, then season. Cut a baguette into thick slices. Toast under a preheated hot broiler for 2–3 minutes on each side until starting to get crisp. Remove and cool a little, but leave the broiler on. Spread some of the crab mixture onto each slice of bread. Scatter with ¼ cup each grated Gruyère and grated Parmesan cheese. Cook under the broiler for 3–5 minutes, or until bubbling and melted.

Crispy Crab Bites

Mix together 11 oz brown and white crabmeat and a generous ½ cup cream cheese. Stir in a splash of Tabasco sauce, 1–2 teaspoons fresh lemon juice, and season with salt and pepper. Melt 3½ tablespoons butter and whisk with 3 tablespoons olive oil. Brush over 1 sheet of filo pastry, place another sheet of filo on top and brush again, then repeat once more so that you have 3 layers. Cut into 3 long strips, then cut each strip in half. Place a heaped teaspoon of the crab mixture at the bottom of each strip, fold over to make a triangle and keep folding to enclose the filling. Place on a cookie sheet, brush the surface of each parcel with the rest of the oil mixture, and place in a preheated oven at 400°F. Bake for 15 minutes, or until golden and crisp, and serve.

Mini Garlicky Cod Bites

Serves 4–6

3 tablespoons butter, softened

2 garlic cloves, crushed

2 tablespoons finely grated Parmesan

handful of flat-leaf parsley, chopped

1 lb thick cod fillet, skinned

6 tablespoons olive oil, plus extra for oiling and drizzling

¾ cup dried bread crumbs

salt and pepper

- Mix together the butter, garlic, Parmesan, and parsley in a small bowl.

- Cut the cod into pieces about 1 inch thick, then season. Use a small, sharp knife to make a little pocket in the center of each piece of fish. Push a small spoonful of butter inside each pocket. Close up the pockets so no butter is visible.

- Place the oil and bread crumbs on separate plates. Dip each piece of fish in the oil until really well coated, then roll in the bread crumbs to coat. Place on an oiled baking pan and drizzle with more oil. Place in a preheated oven at 400°F for 15 minutes, or until golden, crisp, and cooked through, and serve.

 ### Lemon and Garlic Fried Cod

Cut 1 lb thick cod fillet into pieces about 1 inch thick and dust with all-purpose flour. Heat 1 tablespoon olive oil in a large, nonstick skillet and cook the cod for 5 minutes, turning once, or until golden and just cooked through. Add 1 sliced garlic clove along with 2 tablespoons butter and swirl around the pan. Cook for a further minute. Squeeze the juice of ½ lemon onto the fish and scatter with chopped parsley to serve.

 ### Baked Cod with Garlicky Pesto

Butter In a food processor, pulse together a large handful of fresh basil, 2 crushed garlic cloves, 2 tablespoons grated Parmesan cheese, and 1 tablespoon pine nuts until smooth. Add 3½ tablespoons softened butter and pulse until well combined. Transfer the butter mixture to a sheet of foil, then roll it up in the foil into a cigar shape and twist the ends to enclose. Chill in the freezer while you cook the cod. Place 4 x 6 oz cod fillets on a lightly greased baking pan. Place in a preheated oven at 400°F for 10 minutes. Unwrap the butter and cut into slices. Place a slice on top of each cod fillet and return to the oven for 2–3 minutes, or until the fish is cooked through and the butter has started to melt.

QuickCook
Family Meals

Recipes listed by cooking time

10

30 Beer-Battered Cod and Chips

Serves 4

2 tablespoons butter
2 scallions, minced
2 cups frozen peas
1 scant cup vegetable stock
1¼ cups all-purpose flour
1½ cups beer
vegetable oil, for deep-frying
½ lb round red or round white
   potatoes, peeled and cut into
   chips ½ inch thick
4 cod fillets, each weighing about
   6 oz, skin on
2 tablespoons cornstarch
salt and pepper
lemon wedges, to serve

- Heat the butter in a small saucepan and cook the scallions for 2 minutes until softened. Add the peas and stock and simmer for 3 minutes. Roughly mash and keep warm.

- Meanwhile beat together the flour and beer, then season well with salt and pepper.

- Fill a large, deep saucepan over medium heat one-third full with oil. When a cube of bread dropped in the oil turns brown in 30 seconds the oil is ready. Dry the chips in paper towels. Deep-fry in batches for 5 minutes, or until golden.

- Season the fish and dust with the cornstarch. Dip into the batter until coated, shake off any excess, and deep-fry in batches for 7 minutes, using long-handled tongs to turn the fish over. Drain on paper towels. Keep warm in the oven. Increase the heat until a cube of bread dropped in the oil browns in 15 seconds. Deep-fry the chips again in batches for 2 minutes, or until crisp and golden. Serve the fish and chips with the mashed peas and lemon wedges on the side.

---

1 Broiled Cod with Pea Salad

Brush 1 tablespoon olive oil all over 4 x 6 oz cod steaks. Cook on a smoking hot ridged griddle pan for 3–5 minutes on each side. Meanwhile, whisk together 3 tablespoons olive oil and 1 tablespoon white wine vinegar. Season. Stir in some chopped chives. Boil ¾ cup frozen peas for 3 minutes. Drain, cool under the cold running water, and toss with the dressing. Slice 4 Little Gem lettuces into wedges and serve with the peas and cod.

2 Crispy Cod with Tartare Crust

Spread 1 tablespoon tartare sauce over each of 4 x 6 oz skinless cod fillets. Arrange on a baking pan and scatter evenly with ¾ cup bread crumbs. Place in a preheated oven at 400°F for 12–15 minutes, or until cooked through and crisp. Serve with oven-baked fries.

20 Asian Seafood Noodles

Serves 4

3½ oz pork tenderloin, cut into thin strips

2 tablespoons sweet chili sauce

2 tablespoons vegetable oil

1 red pepper, sliced

4 scallions, sliced

2 garlic cloves, crushed

1 teaspoon minced fresh ginger root

1 tablespoon curry paste

3½ oz raw squid rings

5 oz cooked peeled small shrimp

10 oz fresh egg noodles

2 tablespoons soy sauce

½ cup bean sprouts

- Toss the pork strips in the sweet chili sauce. Cook under a preheated hot broiler for 7 minutes, turning once, until cooked through, then keep warm.

- Heat a wok over high heat until smoking, then pour in the oil. Stir-fry the red pepper for 1 minute. Add the scallions, garlic, and ginger and sauté, then stir in the curry paste followed by the squid rings. Stir-fry for 1 minute, or until the squid is cooked through.

- Add the shrimp, noodles, soy sauce, bean sprouts, and pork to the wok, with a splash of boiling water if necessary. Sauté until heated through, then divide into bowls and serve.

 Spicy Shrimp Noodles

Heat 1 tablespoon curry paste in a large saucepan. Add 2 diced scallions and 2 grated carrots and cook for 2 minutes until softened. Add 5 cups vegetable stock, 10 oz fresh stir-fry egg noodles, and 7 oz cooked peeled jumbo shrimp. Heat through, then scatter with sesame seeds to serve.

Pork with Shrimp Noodles

Rub 3 tablespoons hoisin sauce all over a 14½ oz piece of pork tenderloin. Place on a lightly oiled baking pan. Drizzle with 1 tablespoon vegetable oil and roast in a preheated oven at 425°F for 20–25 minutes, or until cooked through. Meanwhile, heat 1 tablespoon vegetable oil in a wok. Add 4 sliced scallions, 2 crushed garlic cloves, and 1 teaspoon minced fresh ginger root. Stir-fry for 1 minute. Add 5 oz cooked peeled shrimp and 10 oz fresh egg noodles. Heat through. Whisk together 2 tablespoons soy sauce, 1 tablespoon sweet chili sauce, 1–2 teaspoons fresh lime juice, and 1 teaspoon cornstarch. Add to the wok with 3 tablespoons water. Cook, stirring occasionally, until thickened. Cut the pork into thick slices and serve it with the stir-fried noodles.

Trout and Bacon Hash

Serves 3–4

1 lb new potatoes, halved
1 tablespoon butter
¾ lb trout fillets
4 slices bacon
3 tablespoons olive oil
1 onion, thinly sliced
salt and pepper
handful of flat-leaf parsley,
   chopped, to garnish

- Cook the potatoes in a saucepan of lightly salted boiling water for about 10 minutes, or until just tender, then drain.

- Meanwhile, dot the butter over the trout, season, and cook under a preheated hot broiler for 7–10 minutes, or until cooked through. Remove from the broiler and set aside, keeping the broiler on. Cook the bacon under the broiler until crisp then set aside to cool. When the fish is cool enough to handle, discard the skin and break the flesh into large flakes.

- Heat 2 tablespoons of the oil in a large skillet. Add the onion and cook for 5 minutes, or until softened. Put the remaining oil in the skillet and add the potatoes. Cook until browned and crisp all over. Crumble the bacon into pieces, add to the pan with the trout, and heat through. Scatter with the chopped parsley to serve.

 Bacon and Smoked Trout Gnocchi

Cook 4 slices of bacon under a preheated hot broiler until crisp. Meanwhile, cook 13 oz potato gnocchi according to the package instructions. Drain and mix with 5 oz skinless smoked trout fillets, broken into chunks, 1 teaspoon wholegrain mustard, and 2 tablespoons olive oil. Crumble the bacon over everything to serve.

 Trout and Bacon Hash with Poached Eggs Prepare the hash as above. While the trout and bacon are cooking, heat a small saucepan of water until simmering. Use a spoon and vigorously stir the water to make a whirlpool in the pan. Crack 1 egg into a small cup and gently slide into the center of the whirlpool. Cook for 3–4 minutes until just cooked through. Remove from pan and gently pat dry with paper towels. Keep warm. Repeat with another 2 or 3 eggs, depending on whether you are serving 3 or 4 people. Place a poached egg on top of each serving of the hash.

Honey Mustard Salmon

Serves 4

4 salmon fillets, weighing about
  5 oz each
olive oil, for greasing
2 tablespoons wholegrain mustard
2 tablespoons clear honey
handful of dill, chopped
salt and pepper

- Place the salmon on a lightly greased baking pan or ovenproof dish and season with salt and pepper. Mix together the mustard, honey, and dill and drizzle it over the salmon.

- Place in a preheated oven at 425°F for 8 minutes, or until cooked through. Serve with some new potatoes and a cucumber salad.

 ### Mustard Salmon Burgers

In a food processor, pulse 1 lb skinless salmon fillets to a rough paste. Mix with a handful of bread crumbs and 1 beaten egg. Lightly wet your hands, then shape into 4 patties. Heat 1 tablespoon vegetable oil in a skillet and cook for 5–7 minutes on each side, or until cooked through. Meanwhile, mix together ¼ cup mayonnaise, 1 tablespoon wholegrain mustard, and 2 teaspoons chopped dill. Place each salmon burger in a toasted hamburger bun. Set some cucumber slices on top and a dollop of mayonnaise to serve.

 ### Salmon with Mustard

Hollandaise Place 4 x 4 oz thin salmon fillets on a lightly oiled baking pan, drizzle with 2 tablespoons olive oil, and season with salt and pepper. Place in a preheated oven at 250°F for 25–30 minutes until just cooked through. Meanwhile, crack 2 egg yolks into a heatproof bowl set snugly over a saucepan of simmering water. Add 1–2 teaspoons fresh lemon juice and then slowly whisk in a scant ½ cup melted butter until the sauce has thickened. Stir in 1 teaspoon wholegrain mustard and more lemon juice to taste. Serve with the salmon.

30 Salmon Fishcakes with Dill Sauce

Serves 4

14½ oz potatoes, peeled
  and cubed
3 tablespoons olive oil
1 lb skinless salmon fillet
1 tablespoon chopped dill
finely grated zest of 1 lemon
all-purpose flour, for dusting
1 egg, beaten
¾ cup dried bread crumbs
salt and pepper
green salad, to serve

For the dill sauce

3 tablespoons mayonnaise
3 tablespoons plain yogurt
handful of dill, chopped
1 cornichon, sliced

- Cook the potatoes in a saucepan of lightly salted boiling water for 12 minutes until soft. Drain well and mash roughly.

- Meanwhile, rub 1 teaspoon of the oil all over the salmon and season well with salt and pepper. Cook under a preheated hot broiler for 10 minutes, or until cooked through. Leave to cool a little, then break into large flakes. Mix together the ingredients for the sauce.

- Mix together the potato, salmon, dill, and lemon zest. Lightly wet your hands, then shape the mixture into 8 fishcakes. Dust each fishcake with a little flour, dip into the egg, and finally dip into the bread crumbs until well coated.

- Heat the remaining oil in a large, nonstick skillet. Cook the fishcakes for 3–4 minutes on each side, or until golden and crisp. Serve with a green salad and the dill sauce.

 Easy Salmon and Potato Salad

Discard the skin and any bones from 1 x 5 oz hot-smoked salmon fillet, then flake. Stir into a 1 lb container ready-made creamy plain potato salad along with a handful of chopped dill and 1 sliced cornichon. Serve with strips of pita bread that have been toasted until crisp.

 Moroccan-Style Salmon Cakes

Place 1 scant cup couscous in a heatproof bowl. Add 1 cup boiling water and season with salt. Cover with plastic wrap and leave to stand for about 7 minutes until swelled. Uncover and leave to cool a little, then mix with 2 x 6 oz cans salmon or tuna, drained , 1 beaten egg, a handful of cilantro, chopped, and 1–2 teaspoons harissa spice mix. Lightly wet your hands, then form the mixture into 4 fishcakes. Heat 1 tablespoon olive oil in a large, nonstick skillet. Add the fishcakes and cook for 3–5 minutes on each side until browned, then serve.

Smoked Haddock and Corn Chowder

Serves 4

1 tablespoon butter
1 small onion, chopped
2½ cups milk
¼ cup heavy cream
¾ lb new potatoes, halved
3 slices bacon, chopped
2 skinless smoked haddock fillets,
  weighing about 5 oz each
¾ cup whole kernel sweet corn
salt and pepper
handful of chives, chopped, to
  garnish
crusty bread, to serve

- Melt the butter in a large, heavy saucepan. Add the onion and cook for a few minutes until softened. Pour in the milk and cream, add the potatoes, and season with salt and pepper. Bring to a boil and cook for 10 minutes.

- Meanwhile, cook the bacon under a preheated hot broiler for 7–10 minutes until crisp, then set aside.

- Add the fish fillets to the milk and potato mixture and cook for 3 minutes. Stir through the corn, gently breaking up the fish, and cook for a further 3 minutes, or until the fish is cooked through. Ladle into serving bowls, then scatter with the bacon and chopped chives. Serve with crusty bread.

Griddled Haddock and Creamed Corn

Heat a ridged griddle pan until smoking hot. Rub 1 tablespoon vegetable oil all over 4 x 5 oz haddock fillets. Cook in the pan, skin-side down, for 5 minutes. Turn over and cook for a further 3 minutes until cooked through. Meanwhile, heat 2 tablespoons butter in a saucepan. Add a drained 8½ oz can whole kernel sweet corn and heat through. Stir in 3 tablespoons crème fraîche. Scatter with chopped chives and serve with the haddock.

Haddock with Corn and Clam Sauce

Cut 4 peeled potatoes into chunks. Cook in a saucepan of lightly salted boiling water for 12–15 minutes, or until soft then keep them warm. Meanwhile, heat 1 tablespoon vegetable oil in a skillet and cook 1 diced shallot for 5 minutes until softened. Pour in ½ scant cup dry white wine and cook until reduced by half. Add 3½ oz cleaned live clams, cover, and cook for about 5 minutes, or until the clams have opened. Discard any that remain closed. Stir in a generous ½ cup drained canned whole kernel sweet corn and ¼ cup heavy cream. Keep warm. Rub a little vegetable oil over 4 x 5 oz smoked haddock fillets and cook under a preheated hot broiler for 3–5 minutes on each side, or until cooked through. Place 4 slices of pancetta under the broiler with the fish and cook until crisp. Arrange the potatoes and haddock on a deep serving plate, pour the sauce over the fish, and arrange the pancetta slices on top to serve.

3 ◐ Spicy Tuna Empanadas

Serves 4

12 oz sheet puff pastry
6 oz can tuna in water, drained
½ cup ready-made tomato sauce
1 teaspoon smoked paprika
1 ready-roasted red pepper, diced
1 egg yolk, beaten
salt and pepper

- Use a round cookie cutter or small side plate, about 6 inches in diameter, to cut out 4 rounds from the pastry sheet. Mix together the tuna, tomato sauce, paprika, and red pepper. Spread about 2 tablespoons of the mixture into the center of each pastry round.

- Brush around the edge of each pastry round with a little of the beaten egg yolk. Fold the pastry over, squeeze out any air, and use your finger or a fork to seal the edges. Place on a cookie sheet and brush all over with more of the egg.

- Place in a preheated oven at 400°F for 15 minutes, or until crisp, then serve.

 Spicy Tuna Melts
Mix together a drained 6 oz can tuna in water, ¼ cup mayonnaise, and 1 teaspoon smoked paprika. Lightly toast 4 slices of bread. Spread the tuna mixture onto the toast, then place a slice of cheddar cheese on top. Add a layer of sliced tomatoes and then more cheese. Place under a preheated hot broiler and cook for 3–5 minutes, or until the cheese is melted and bubbling.

 Tuna Steak Salad with Pita Chips
Cut 5 plum tomatoes into wedges and thinly slice ½ red onion. Whisk together 1 tablespoon sherry vinegar and 3 tablespoons olive oil. Toss with the tomato and onion and ½ red chile, minced. Brush olive oil all over 4 x 5 oz tuna steaks and cook on a smoking hot ridged griddle pan for 3–5 minutes on each side, or until cooked through. Meanwhile, brush olive oil over

1 pita bread, split in half, and then cut into pieces. Place under a preheated hot broiler and cook until crisp. Toss the tomato and onion salad with the torn leaves of 1 romaine lettuce. Arrange on a serving plate with the tuna steaks and serve with the pita chips alongside.

2⏰ Salmon Tikka Masala

Serves 4

2 tablespoons vegetable oil
1 onion, sliced
1 garlic clove, crushed
1 teaspoon grated fresh ginger root
1 red pepper, sliced
3 tablespoons tikka masala paste
13½ oz can diced tomatoes
¾ lb salmon fillet, cut into chunks
¼ cup light cream
¼ cup plain yogurt
salt and pepper
handful of cilantro, chopped, to garnish
naan bread, to serve

- Heat the oil in a large saucepan. Add the onion, garlic, and ginger and cook for 3 minutes, or until softened. Add the red pepper and cook for a further 2 minutes. Stir in the tikka masala paste followed by the tomatoes and bring to a boil. Cook for 5 minutes.

- Reduce to a simmer, add the salmon, and season. Cook for 8 minutes, or until cooked through. Stir through the cream and some of the yogurt reserving a little to drizzle on the top just before you scatter the dish with the cilantro. Serve with naan bread.

1⏰ Salmon Tikka Wraps

Mix 3 tablespoons tikka masala paste with 3 tablespoons plain yogurt and spread it all over 4 x 3½ oz thin salmon fillets. Cook under a preheated hot broiler for 7 minutes, or until cooked through. Break the fish into flakes, discarding the skin and any bones. Divide between 4 chapatis. Add some chopped lettuce, cucumber, and more yogurt. Roll up and serve.

3⏰ Salmon with Homemade Masala

Paste Combine 2 tablespoons tomato paste, 1 tablespoon ground cumin, 2 teaspoons ground coriander, 1 teaspoon smoked paprika, and ¼ teaspoon sugar. Heat 2 tablespoons vegetable oil in a saucepan over medium heat. Add 1 diced onion, 1 crushed garlic clove, and 1 teaspoon grated fresh ginger root. Cook for 3 minutes, or until softened. Stir in half the spice paste followed by a 13½ oz can diced tomatoes. Bring to a boil, then simmer for 20 minutes. Meanwhile, mix the remaining paste with 3 tablespoons vegetable oil. Spread over 4 x 3½ oz thin salmon fillets. Cook under a preheated medium broiler for 10 minutes, or until charred and cooked through. Spoon the curry sauce over the salmon and drizzle with some plain yogurt to serve.

FIS-FAMI-NUU

30 Crunchy Sardine Caesar Salad

Serves 4

2 eggs
1 garlic clove, crushed
juice of ½ lemon
½ teaspoon Worcestershire sauce
½ cup extra virgin olive oil
½ cup bread crumbs
¼ cup Parmesan cheese, grated,
  plus extra, shaved, to serve
2 tablespoons milk
8 sardines, filleted and halved
vegetable oil, for deep-frying
1 large romaine lettuce, sliced
salt and pepper

- Crack 1 egg into a saucepan of boiling water and cook for just 45 seconds. Leave to cool a little, then pulse in a food processor with the garlic, lemon juice, and Worcestershire sauce. With the motor running, slowly add the oil in a thin stream until thickened. Season with salt and pepper and set aside.

- Mix together the bread crumbs and Parmesan and place in a large freezer bag. Beat together the remaining egg and the milk. Dip the sardines into the egg mixture until coated, shake off any excess, then place in the freezer bag, seal, and shake until coated.

- Fill a large, deep saucepan one-third full with oil over medium heat. When a cube of bread dropped in the oil turns brown in 15 seconds the oil is ready. Deep-fry the sardines in batches for 3–5 minutes, or until golden and crisp. Drain on paper towels.

- Divide the lettuce among the serving plates. Arrange the sardines on top, then drizzle with the dressing, and shave some Parmesan on top to serve.

---

10 Easy Caesar Salad

Stir 1 crushed garlic clove and ¼ cup grated Parmesan cheese a generous ¼ cup mayonnaise. Tear ¼ baguette into chunks. Toast under a preheated hot broiler. Toss 1 sliced Romaine lettuce with the mayonnaise, toasted chunks of baguette, and a handful of marinated sardines or herrings, or a few anchovies in oil, drained, to serve.

20 Crunchy Fishcake Salad

Drain 2 x 6 oz cans tuna and a 4½ oz pouch smoked tuna. Beat together 2 eggs, then use a little of the egg to mix together the tuna and 1 diced scallion. Lightly wet your hands, then shape the mixture into 4 fishcakes. Dust with all-purpose flour, then dip into the remaining egg and press into ½ cup bread crumbs to coat. Heat 3 tablespoons olive oil in a large, nonstick skillet. Cook the fishcakes for 3–4 minutes on each side, or until golden and crisp. Meanwhile, stir 1 small crushed garlic clove into a scant ½ cup mayonnaise along with 1–2 teaspoons fresh lemon juice, and 2 tablespoons grated Parmesan cheese. Arrange a fishcake and a handful of green salad leaves on each of 4 serving plates. Spoon some mayonnaise on top of each and serve.

Mini Seafood Pizza Bites

Serves 4

4 mini pita breads

2 tablespoons olive oil

1 garlic clove, peeled and halved

scant ½ cup ready-made tomato and basil pasta sauce

1 tablespoon tomato paste

¼ cup cooked peeled shrimp, halved

1 roasted red pepper, torn into strips

4 oz mozzarella cheese, torn into strips

salt and pepper

a few basil leaves, chopped, to garnish

- Split the mini pita breads open and separate the two sides so you have 8 rounds. Drizzle the oil over the insides. Toast, oiled-side up, under a preheated hot broiler for 2–3 minutes, or until crisp. Rub all over with the garlic clove halves.

- Meanwhile, mix together the tomato sauce and tomato paste and season with salt and pepper. Spoon over the toasted sides of the bread. Arrange the shrimp, red pepper, and mozzarella on top. Return them to the broiler and cook for 3–5 minutes, or until the cheese has melted. Scatter with the basil and serve.

 ### Speedy Seafood Pizza

Mix together ½ cup ready-made tomato and basil sauce and 3 tablespoons tomato paste. Place a ready-made pizza crust on a pizza pan and cover with the tomato sauce. Heat 1 tablespoon olive oil in a skillet. Cook ¼ lb raw peeled shrimp, 2 oz raw squid rings, and 1 crushed garlic clove for 3–5 minutes, or until cooked through. Scatter onto the pizza with 1 roasted red pepper and 4 oz mozzarella cheese, both torn into strips. Place in a preheated oven at 400°F for 10 minutes, then serve.

 ### Homemade Seafood Pizzas

In a large bowl, mix together 2 cups white bread flour, 1 teaspoon active yeast granules, and ½ teaspoon salt. Add ¾ cup warm water and 1 tablespoon olive oil. Stir until the mixture comes together into a dough. Knead a couple of times on a floured surface. Divide into 4 balls and roll out as thinly as you can. Place on cookie sheets. Mix together ½ cup ready-made tomato and basil sauce and 3 tablespoons tomato paste and spread it thinly over the pizza crusts. Arrange ¼ lb raw peeled shrimp, 7 oz cleaned live clams on top, then add a layer of ¼ lb mozzarella cheese slices. Scatter with dried red pepper flakes and some dried oregano. Place in a preheated oven at 475°F for 10–15 minutes, or until cooked through. Discard any clams that remain closed after cooking.

Pan-Fried Striped Mullet with Herby Potato Salad

Serves 4

1½ lb new potatoes, halved

5 tablespoons extra virgin olive oil

finely grated zest and
  juice of 1 lemon

4 striped mullet fillets, weighing
  about 5 oz each

4 scallions, sliced

½ red chile, minced

handful of basil and parsley
  leaves, chopped

salt and pepper

- Cook the potatoes in a saucepan of lightly salted boiling water for 12 minutes until tender, then drain and slice thickly. Toss with 4 tablespoons of the oil and the lemon zest and juice, season with salt and pepper, and leave to cool a little.

- Meanwhile, heat the remaining oil in a large skillet. Add the fish fillets skin-side down, season with salt and pepper, and cook for 5 minutes. Turn over and cook for a further 3–5 minutes, or until cooked through.

- Stir the scallions, chile, and herbs through the potatoes and serve with the fish.

Herby Fish Strips with Couscous

Place 2¼ cups couscous in a heatproof bowl. Add 2 cups boiling water, a walnut-sized lum of butter, and season with salt. Cover and leave for 7–10 minutes, or until swollen. Meanwhile, cut 4 x 7 oz striped mullet fillets into thin strips and season. Mix together 2 tablespoons olive oil, ½ red chile, minced, and a handful of basil and flat-leaf parsley, chopped. Toss with the fish. Cook under a preheated hot broiler for 3–5 minutes on each side, or until cooked through. Serve with the couscous and a green salad.

Spiced Fish with Herby Pilaf

Heat 2 tablespoons butter in a large saucepan over medium heat. Add 1 diced onion and 1 minced garlic clove and cook until softened. Add 1 generous cup basmati rice, stirring it around to coat, then pour in 3¼ cups hot vegetable stock. Bring to a boil and cook for about 10 minutes, or until the liquid has nearly boiled off and small craters appear in the surface of the rice. Cover with a tightly fitting lid and leave to stand for 10 minutes. Meanwhile, rub 1 tablespoon olive oil all over 4 x 7 oz striped mullet fillets, then dust with ½ teaspoon each ground cumin and paprika. Place under a preheated hot broiler and cook for 7–10 minutes, or until cooked through. Stir a handful of basil and flat-leaf parsley, chopped, through the rice along with the finely grated zest of ½ lemon and 1–2 teaspoons fresh lemon juice. Serve the rice alongside the fish.

30 Crispy Salmon and Pesto Parcels

Serves 4

3½ tablespoons butter, melted
¼ cup olive oil
4 large sheets of filo pastry
4 skinless salmon fillets, weighing
about 5 oz each
¼ cup fresh green pesto
¼ cup cream cheese
salt and pepper
tomato salad, to serve

- Stir together the melted butter and oil. Use a pastry brush to brush the mixture all over 1 sheet of filo pastry (cover the remaining pastry with a damp but not wet piece of paper towel).

- Place 1 salmon fillet at one end of the sheet and season with salt and pepper. Mix together the pesto and cream cheese and spread a little over the top of the salmon. Fold over the ends of the pastry, then roll up to enclose the salmon. Place it, seam-side down (you may have to trim the edge), on a cookie sheet and brush all over with more of the butter mixture. Repeat with the remaining salmon fillets.

- Place in a preheated oven at 425°F for 15 minutes, or until browned and crisp. Serve with a tomato salad.

10 Smoked Salmon, Cheese, and Pesto

Rotolos Spread 3 tablespoons cream cheese all over each of 2 wraps. Scatter with 1 slice of smoked salmon, cut into strips, and drizzle with 2 teaspoons fresh green pesto. Roll the wraps up tightly, then use a sharp knife to trim the ends and slice into bite-size pieces. Serve with a mixed leaf salad.

20 Salmon, Pea, and Pesto Soup

Melt 1 tablespoon butter in a saucepan. Add 1 diced onion and 1 crushed garlic clove and cook for about 5 minutes, or until softened. Pour in 3¼ cups chicken stock and bring to a boil. Leave to simmer for 2 minutes, then add 1 diced zucchini and cook for a further 1–2 minutes. Stir through ¼ cup frozen peas and ¼ cup fresh green pesto and cook for a further 3 minutes. Remove the skin from a 6 oz hot-smoked salmon fillet and break into chunks. Add to the soup and heat through. Swirl 2 tablespoons crème fraîche into the top of the soup to serve.

20 Sweet and Sour Fish

Serves 4

vegetable oil, for frying
1 onion, sliced
1 tablespoon thinly sliced fresh
    ginger root
3 garlic cloves, crushed
1 red pepper, sliced
2 tablespoons tomato ketchup
2 tablespoons rice vinegar
2 tablespoons superfine sugar
1 tablespoon soy sauce
1 teaspoon cornstarch
¾ cup self-rising flour
1 egg, beaten
13 oz sea bass fillet, skinned, if
    you like, and cut into chunks
2 scallions, sliced
salt and pepper

- Heat 1 tablespoon oil in a wok. Add the onion and stir-fry for 2 minutes. Add the ginger, garlic, and red pepper and stir-fry for 2 minutes until softened. Mix together the ketchup, vinegar, sugar, soy sauce, ¾ cup water, and the cornstarch until smooth. Stir into the wok and cook for 3–5 minutes until thickened. Keep warm.

- Fill a large, deep saucepan one-third full with oil over medium heat. The oil is ready when a cube of bread dropped in the oil turns brown in 15 seconds the oil is ready. Beat together the flour, egg, and ½ cup iced water (don't worry if there are still a few lumps), then season well with salt and pepper. Coat the fish in the batter, shake off any excess, and deep-fry in 2 batches for 3–4 minutes, or until golden brown all over. Drain on paper towels.

- Stir the fish into the sauce, then serve immediately scattered with sliced scallions.

---

10 Sweet and Sour Shrimp Noodles

Stir-fry a 10 oz package of stir-fry vegetables in a wok in a little vegetable oil over high heat. Add 3½ oz cooked peeled shrimp and 10 oz fresh egg noodles. Mix 2 tablespoons each tomato ketchup, rice vinegar, and superfine sugar, 1 tablespoon soy sauce, ¾ cup water, and 1 teaspoon cornstarch in a bowl. Add to the wok and cook, stirring, for 3–5 minutes, or until thickened, and serve.

30 Marinated Sweet and Sour Fish

Marinate a 13 oz sea bass fillet, skinned and cut into chunks, in 1 tablespoon each soy sauce and sherry for 15 minutes. Meanwhile, stir-fry 1 sliced onion, 3 crushed garlic cloves, and 1 tablespoon thinly sliced fresh ginger root in 1 tablespoon vegetable oil for 5 minutes, or until softened. Stir in 3 tablespoons each soy sauce, sherry, and water along with 1 teaspoon clear honey. Simmer until sticky, set aside, and keep warm. Fill a large, deep saucepan one-third full with oil. When a cube of bread dropped into the oil turns brown in 15 seconds the oil is ready. Beat together ¾ cup self-rising flour, 1 beaten egg, and ½ cup iced water. Season well with salt and pepper. Pat the fish dry and dip it in the batter to coat. Deep-fry in 2 batches for 3–4 minutes, or until golden brown. Drizzle with the sauce to serve.

 Crispy Lemon Shrimp Skewers

Serves 4

10 oz cooked peeled
   jumbo shrimp
3 tablespoons olive oil
1 cup dried bread crumbs
1 garlic clove, crushed
finely grated zest of 1 lemon
handful of oregano leaves,
   finely chopped
salt and pepper
lemon wedges, to serve

- Pat the shrimp dry with paper towels, then season with salt and pepper, and rub all over with the oil. Thread onto 8 metal skewers.

- Mix together the remaining ingredients and place on a plate. Roll the skewered shrimp in the bread crumb mixture to coat. Place under a hot broiler and cook for 2 minutes. Turn over and cook for a further 1–2 minutes, or until golden, then serve with lemon wedges.

 Sticky Lemon Shrimp Noodles

Cook, then drain 10 oz dried medium egg noodles according to the package instructions. Heat 2 tablespoons vegetable oil in a wok or large skillet over high heat. Add 2 sliced scallions, 2 chopped garlic cloves, 1 teaspoon minced fresh ginger root, 1 sliced red onion, and 2 cups snow peas. Stir-fry for 5 minutes. Add ½ lb raw peeled jumbo shrimp. Stir-fry for 5 minutes until cooked through. Mix 1 teaspoon cornstarch with 2 tablespoons soy sauce, the juice of 1 lemon, 1 tablespoon clear honey, and ¼ cup water. Add to the wok and heat through. Add the noodles, cook for 2 minutes, and serve.

 Fennel, Lemon, and Shrimp Risotto

Heat 1 tablespoon olive oil in a large, deep skillet over medium heat. Add 1 diced onion, 1 diced fennel bulb, and 1 minced garlic clove. Cook for 5–7 minutes, or until softened. Stir in 1½ cups risotto rice until well coated. Pour in ¾ cup dry white wine and boil until reduced. Add about 3¼ pints (about 6¼ cups) hot fish stock, a ladleful at a time, stirring and simmering after each addition until the stock is absorbed before adding the next ladleful. Continue until all the stock is absorbed, about 15–20 minutes. Stir in ½ lb raw peeled jumbo shrimp and cook for a further 5 minutes until the rice is tender and the shrimp are cooked through. Just before serving squeeze in the juice of 1 lemon and stir in ¼ cup grated Parmesan cheese and 1 tablespoon butter.

Cod with Lemon, Basil, and Sun-Dried Tomato Crust

Serves 4

4 thick cod fillets, weighing about
5 oz each

2 tablespoons olive oil, plus extra
for greasing

¾ cup bread crumbs

4 sun-dried tomatoes, diced

finely grated zest of 1 lemon

handful of basil, chopped

salt and pepper

- Season the cod, then place on a lightly greased baking pan. Rub 1 tablespoon of the oil all over the top of the fish.

- Mix together all the remaining ingredients. Press on top of each fish fillet, then drizzle with the remaining oil. Place in a preheated oven at 400°F for 12–15 minutes, or until the fish is lightly crisp and cooked through. Serve with potatoes and a tomato salad.

Tomato Pesto Cod Bites

Cut 4 x 5 oz thick cod fillets into small pieces. Whisk together 1 tablespoon olive oil and 2 tablespoons sun-dried tomato pesto, then toss with the fish. Place ¾ cups bread crumbs and a handful of basil, chopped, in a large freezer bag, add the cod pieces, seal well, and shake until coated. Heat 2 tablespoons olive oil in a skillet and cook the cod for 5 minutes, turning often, until cooked through, then serve.

Cod with Lemon Pesto and Tomatoes

In a food processor, pulse together a large handful of fresh basil, ¼ cup grated Parmesan cheese, 5 tablespoons extra virgin olive oil, and the finely grated zest of ½ lemon until you have a paste. Heat a small dry skillet and add 2 tablespoons pine nuts. Cook until lightly browned all over. Set aside to cool a little then roughly chop and add to the paste. Place 4 x 5 oz thick cod fillets on a baking pan and spread the paste

all over them. Thinly slice 2 tomatoes and arrange them on top of the cod. Place in a preheated oven at 400°F for 12–15 minutes, or until the fish is cooked through.

30 Salmon, Pea, and Dill Tortilla

Serves 4

¾ lb potatoes, peeled and thickly
  sliced
5 oz skinless salmon fillet
6 eggs, beaten
handful of dill, chopped
¾ cup frozen peas
1 scallion, sliced
1 tablespoon vegetable oil
salt and pepper
mixed salad leaves, to serve

- Cook the potatoes in a saucepan of lightly salted boiling water for 10 minutes until tender, then carefully drain.

- Meanwhile, place the salmon in a small saucepan. Cover with boiling water and leave to simmer for 7 minutes until the fish flakes easily. Drain, then break into large flakes.

- Mix together the eggs, dill, peas, and scallion, then season. Heat the oil in an 8 inch nonstick skillet. Stir the potatoes and salmon into the egg mixture, then add to the skillet. Cook over very low heat for 10–15 minutes, or until just set. Cut into wedges and serve with a mixed leaf salad.

10 Pea and Salmon Omelets

Boil ¼ cup frozen peas for 3 minutes, or until cooked through, then drain. Beat 4 eggs together with some dill. Heat 1 tablespoon butter in a small skillet. Add one-quarter of the egg mixture and swirl around the pan. Cook for 1 minute until the mixture is starting to set, then sprinkle with 1 teaspoon grated Parmesan cheese, a few of the peas, and a slice of smoked salmon, cut into strips. Fold the omelet over and serve. Repeat with the remaining egg mixture.

20 Pea and Smoked Salmon Soup

Heat 1 tablespoon butter in a saucepan over medium heat. Add 1 diced onion and cook for 5 minutes until softened. Pour in 3¼ cups hot chicken stock. Bring to a boil, then simmer and add 1¼ cups frozen peas and a mint sprig. Cook for 3 minutes until the peas are tender. Use a stick blender to pulse until smooth. Stir in 2 tablespoons crème fraîche. Cut 3 oz smoked salmon into shreds and scatter onto the soup to serve.

FIS-FAMI-BUH

20 Plaice Florentine

Serves 4

1 tablespoon butter, plus extra for
  greasing
1 tablespoon all-purpose flour
¾ cup milk
½ cup cheddar cheese, grated
5 oz frozen spinach
2 large American plaice fillets,
  weighing about 6 oz each,
  halved to make 4 thin fillets
¼ cup Parmesan cheese, grated
salt and pepper
mashed potatoes, to serve

- Melt the butter in a saucepan. Stir in the flour and cook for 2 minutes. Slowly whisk in the milk until smooth. Bring to a boil, whisking, then simmer for a few minutes until thickened. Take off the heat, stir in the cheese, and season with salt and pepper.

- Place the spinach in a sieve and pour boiling water over it until it has thawed. Drain well, then roughly chop. Place the fish on a lightly greased baking pan. Spread a layer of spinach on top of each fillet, then drizzle with some of the white sauce. Sprinkle with the Parmesan.

- Place in a preheated oven at 400°F for 10–12 minutes, or until the fish is just cooked through. Serve immediately with mashed potatoes.

---

10 Plaice with Simple Parsley Sauce

Smear a little butter over 4 x 6 oz American plaice fillets. Cook under a preheated hot broiler for 7–10 minutes, or until just cooked through. Meanwhile, mix ¼ cup crème fraîche with a large handful of parsley, chopped, and a little milk to loosen. Spoon this onto the fish and serve alongside some lightly cooked spinach and mashed canned lima beans warmed through in a saucepan.

30 Creamy Spinach and Plaice Pie

Place 10 oz frozen spinach in a sieve and pour boiling water over it until it is thawed. Squeeze to dry then set in the bottom of a baking dish. Poach 2 large American plaice fillets, weighing about 6 oz each, in a wide pan in ½ cup dry white wine plus enough water to cover for 7–10 minutes, or until cooked through. Remove the fish. Boil the liquid until you have ½ cup left. Melt 2 tablespoons butter in a pan. Stir in ¼ cup all-purpose flour and cook for 2 minutes. Whisk the reduced poaching liquid in followed by a scant cup milk until smooth. Bring to a boil, whisking, then simmer for a few minutes until thickened. Remove from the heat and stir in 2 tablespoons crème fraîche, ¼ cup grated Parmesan cheese, and 1 egg yolk. Place the cooked fish on top of the spinach, pour the sauce on top, and place under a hot broiler. Cook for 3–5 minutes, or until browned.

1 Simple Tuna Pasta

Serves 4

13 oz quick-cook penne
2 oz anchovy fillets in oil
2 garlic cloves, crushed
1 chile, seeded and chopped
  (optional)
6 oz can tuna in water, drained
lemon juice, to taste
handful of flat-leaf parsley,
  chopped
pepper

- Cook the pasta according to the package instructions.

- Meanwhile, drain the anchovies, reserving the oil. Heat a little of the reserved oil in a small skillet. Add the anchovies, garlic and chile, if using, and cook for about 3 minutes until the anchovies have dissolved into the oil. Stir in the tuna and lemon juice to taste, then season with plenty of pepper.

- Drain the pasta, reserving a little of the cooking water. Return to the pan and stir through the tuna sauce and most of the parsley. Add some of the reserved cooking water to loosen the mixture if necessary. Scatter with the remaining parsley to serve.

2 Tuna Ball Pasta

Place a drained 6 oz can tuna in water in a bowl. Add 1 beaten egg and a pinch of dried red pepper flakes. Stir together. Lightly wet your hands, then shape the mixture into small balls. Heat 1 tablespoon olive oil in a skillet over medium heat. Cook the tuna balls for 10 minutes, or until golden all over. Heat a 10½ oz jar tomato and basil pasta sauce in a pan. Add the tuna balls and cook for 5 minutes. Meanwhile, cook 13 oz penne according to the package instructions. Drain and stir through the sauce. Scatter with chopped basil to serve.

3 Tuna and Sweetcorn Pasta Bake

Cook 13 oz dried penne according to the package instructions. Meanwhile, melt 3 tablespoons butter in a saucepan over low heat, stir in a generous ¼ cup all-purpose flour and cook, stirring all the while, for 2 minutes. Slowly whisk in 2½ cups milk until smooth. Bring to a boil, whisking continuously, then simmer until thickened. Drain the pasta and mix it with the sauce and a 6 oz can tuna in water and a drained 8½ oz can whole kernel sweet corn. Pour into a large baking dish, scatter with 1 cup dried bread crumbs and place in a preheated oven at 400°F for 15 minutes until golden.

Fish Tortillas with Avocado Salsa

Serves 4

1 avocado
handful of cilantro, chopped, plus extra to serve
1 tablespoon vegetable oil
1 teaspoon ground cumin
1 teaspoon paprika
handful of thyme, chopped
6 skinless sea robin fillets, weighing about 3½ oz each, cut into strips
8 soft flour tortillas
1 scant cup radishes, thinly sliced
1 lime, cut into wedges
¼ cup sour cream
salt and pepper

- Cut the avocado in half and discard the stone. Peel, then cut the flesh into slices.

- Heat a ridged griddle pan. Mix together the cilantro, the oil, cumin, paprika, and thyme, then season with salt and pepper. Rub the mixture all over the fish strips, then cook on the griddle pan for 2 minutes on each side or until cooked through.

- Meanwhile, warm the tortillas in a microwave or in the oven according to the package instructions.

- Set out the avocado, radish slices, lime wedges, and sour cream on a serving board or platter. Place a little of the fish, avocado, vegetables, and 1–2 teaspoons fresh lime juice in each tortilla. Put some sour cream and a few cilantro sprigs on top, then roll the tortilla up to eat.

Spicy Tuna Tortilla Wraps

Mix together a drained 6 oz can tuna in water, 1 diced tomato, 1 diced red pepper, ¼ cup plus 1 tablespoon mayonnaise, and 2 drops of Tabasco. Spread the mixture evenly over 4 soft flour tortillas, roll up and serve.

Fish Tortillas with Pepper Salsa

Rub 2 red peppers and 1 red chile with olive oil. Cook under a hot broiler for 10–15 minutes, or until blackened all over. Seal in a freezer bag for 5 minutes. Meanwhile, mix together 2 tablespoons chopped cilantro, 1 tablespoon vegetable oil, 1 teaspoon each ground cumin and paprika, and a handful of thyme, chopped. Season with salt and pepper. Rub all over 4 x 3½ oz skinless sea robin fillets. Cook on a hot ridged griddle pan for 2 minutes on each side. Warm 6 soft flour tortillas according to the package instructions. Peel the skin off of the peppers and chile, discard the core and seeds, and dice. Mix with 1 diced shallot, 2 tablespoons olive oil, and 2 teaspoons sherry vinegar. Wrap the fish and salsa in the tortillas.

3⏱ Fish Pie

Serves 4

1½ lb potatoes, peeled and cut
into small chunks
1 scant cup crème fraîche
2 tablespoons butter, plus extra
for greasing
1 tablespoon olive oil
¾ lb baby spinach
4 eggs
13 oz skinless pollock or other
white fish fillet, cut into large
chunks
handful of flat-leaf parsley,
chopped
salt and pepper

- Cook the potatoes in a saucepan of lightly salted boiling water for 8–10 minutes, or until soft. Drain and mash with 4 tablespoons of the crème fraîche and the butter, then season with salt and pepper.

- Meanwhile, heat the oil in a large skillet, add the spinach and a splash of water, and cook until wilted. Drain really well.

- Arrange the spinach in the bottom of a greased baking dish, leaving 4 gaps for the eggs. Crack an egg into each gap and scatter with the fish. Mix together the remaining crème fraîche with 5 tablespoons water and the parsley, season, and then spoon over the dish. Then evenly spread the mashed potatoes on top.

- Place in a preheated oven at 425°F for about 15 minutes, or until golden and bubbling.

1⏱ Fish Pie Fillets

Blend ¾ cup cream cheese with a handful of flat-leaf parsley, chopped. Place 3½ oz frozen spinach in a sieve. Pour in boiling water until the spinach thaws, then drain well and finely chop. Spread onto 4 x 4 oz thin white fish fillets, then add a layer of cream cheese. Scatter with ½ cup dried bread crumbs. Place under a preheated hot broiler and cook for 7 minutes, or until the fish is cooked through, then serve.

2⏱ Quick Crispy Fish Pie

Melt 2 tablespoons butter and mix with 3 tablespoons olive oil. Brush onto 1 sheet of filo pastry, place another sheet of filo on top and brush again, then repeat once more until have 3 layers. Loosely bunch up the pastry so it will fit on top of a baking dish. Transfer to a cookie sheet and place in a preheated oven at 425°F for 10–15 minutes, or until crisp. Meanwhile, blend ¾ cup crème fraîche, a handful of flat-leaf parsley, chopped, and 5 tablespoons water together. Place a 13 oz skinless haddock fillet, cut into large chunks, into a saucepan, cover with the crème fraîche mixture, and simmer for 7–10 minutes until cooked through. Place 7 oz frozen spinach in a sieve. Pour boiling water over it until it wilts, then drain and arrange in the bottom of a baking dish. Spoon the fish mixture onto the spinach and place the baked filo pastry on top to serve.

Broiled Hake Steaks with a Lemony Bacon Dressing

Serves 4

2 tablespoons olive oil

4 hake steaks, weighing about 6 oz each

2 tablespoons butter

2 strips bacon, finely sliced

finely grated zest and juice of 1 lemon

handful of flat-leaf parsley, chopped

salt and pepper

- Rub 1 tablespoon of the oil all over the hake steaks and season them with salt and pepper. Cook in a smoking-hot ridged griddle pan for 5 minutes. Turn them over and cook for a further 3 minutes, or until just cooked through.

- Meanwhile, heat the remaining oil in a skillet with the butter. Add the bacon and cook for 5–7 minutes until crisp. Stir in the lemon zest and juice and the parsley. Place the fish on serving plates, spoon the sauce onto them, and serve.

 Fish Finger and Bacon Sandwich

Place 8 fish fingers on a baking pan in a preheated oven at 450°F for 12–15 minutes, or until crisp and brown, turning halfway through cooking. Meanwhile, cook 4 slices of bacon under a hot broiler for 5 minutes on each side until crisp. Mix together the juice of ½ lemon and ¼ cup mayonnaise. Spread the mayonnaise onto 4 slices of white bread. Place 2 fish fingers, a slice of bacon, and a handful of chopped lettuce onto the mayonnaise and cover with another slice of bread. Cut in half and serve with potato chips.

 Roasted Hake with Bacon Lentils

Cook 2¼ cups Puy lentils according to the package instructions, then drain. Meanwhile, heat 1 tablespoon olive oil in a skillet over medium heat. Add 1 diced onion and 1 crushed garlic clove and cook for 5 minutes, or until soft. Remove from the pan, add 4 slices of bacon, cut into matchsticks, and cook for 5 minutes until crisp. Return the onion to the pan along with the lentils and a splash of water and cook together for 5 minutes. Squeeze in the juice of 1 lemon and add plenty of chopped flat-leaf parsley. While the lentil mixture is cooking, rub 1 tablespoon olive oil all over 4 x 5 oz hake steaks and season with salt and pepper. Cook under a hot broiler for 5 minutes. Turn the fish over and cook for a further 3 minutes, or until just cooked through. Serve with the lentils.

30 Salmon and Leek Cannelloni

Serves 4

2 cups hot vegetable or fish stock
3 leeks, thinly sliced
2 salmon fillets, each weighing
about 5 oz, cut into chunks
1 scant cup crème fraîche
8 fresh lasagne sheets
½ cup dried bread crumbs
salt and pepper

- Pour half the hot stock over the leeks in a saucepan and boil for 5 minutes, or until soft. Pour the remaining stock over the salmon in a separate saucepan and simmer for 5 minutes, or until the fish flakes easily. Drain both, reserving the stock. Mix the stock with the crème fraîche. Flake the fish, discarding the skin and any bones.

- Stir together the leeks and salmon with 6 tablespoons of the crème fraîche mixture to loosen, then season. Place some of the mixture along one long side of a lasagne sheet. Roll up and place, seam-side down, in a baking dish. Repeat with the remaining lasagne sheets. Pour over the remaining crème fraîche mixture and sprinkle with the bread crumbs.

- Place in a preheated oven at 400°F for 15–20 minutes, or until golden and cooked through.

10 Leek and Salmon Linguine

Cook 13 oz dried linguine according to the package instructions, adding 3 thinly sliced leeks for the last 5 minutes of cooking. Drain and then stir through 3½ oz chopped smoked salmon and 5 tablespoons crème fraîche before serving.

20 Salmon with a Creamy Leek

Topping Heat 2 tablespoons butter with a little water in a saucepan, add 3 thinly sliced leeks, and cook for 10 minutes or until soft. Stir in a scant ½ cup crème fraîche and 1 teaspoon wholegrain mustard. Place 4 x 5 oz salmon fillets on a baking pan, skin-side down. Spread the leek mixture on top. Cook under a preheated hot broiler for 7–10 minutes, or until cooked through.

30 New Orleans Jambalaya

Serves 4

2 tablespoons vegetable oil

6 oz andouille, kabanos, or other smoked sausage, sliced

1 onion, diced

2 celery sticks, chopped

1 green pepper, chopped

2 garlic cloves, minced

½ teaspoon cayenne

1 generous cup white long-grain rice

1¼ cups canned diced tomatoes

2 cups fish or chicken stock

1 bay leaf

leaves from 1 thyme sprig, chopped

10 oz raw peeled jumbo shrimp

Tabasco sauce, to taste

salt and pepper

· Heat the oil in a large, heavy saucepan. Add the sausage and cook for 3 minutes until browned. Add the onion, celery, green pepper, and garlic and cook until softened. Add the cayenne followed by the rice and stir around the pan until well coated.

· Add the tomatoes to the pan, followed by the stock and herbs, then season with salt and pepper. Bring to a boil, then cover and simmer for 15 minutes. Stir in the shrimp, add a few drops of Tabasco sauce, and leave to cook for a further 3–5 minutes until cooked through.

 New Orleans Skewers

Thread 5 oz cooked chunks of chorizo, 5 oz cooked jumbo shrimp, 1 thickly sliced green pepper, and a handful of cherry tomatoes onto metal skewers. Rub all over with olive oil and dust with cayenne. Place under a preheated hot broiler and cook for 2–3 minutes on each side, then serve.

 New Orleans-Style Spaghetti

Heat 1 tablespoon olive oil in a saucepan. Add 4 oz sliced chorizo, cook for 3 minutes, then transfer to a plate. Add 1 diced onion and 2 crushed garlic cloves to the pan. Cook for 3 minutes then stir in 1 tablespoon tomato paste, ¼ teaspoon of sugar, a 13½ oz can diced tomatoes, and 1 scant cup water. Bring to a boil, then simmer for 8 minutes. Pulse until smooth with a hand-held immersion blender. Return the chorizo to the pan with 1 roasted pepper, cut into pieces, and 5 oz cooked peeled jumbo shrimp. Heat through. Meanwhile, cook 13 oz dried spaghetti according to the package instructions. Drain, then toss with the sauce and serve immediately.

20 Smoked Haddock Rarebit

Serves 4

10 oz smoked haddock fillet
1 scant cup milk
1 tablespoon butter
1 tablespoon all-purpose flour
2 tablespoons ale (optional)
generous ½ cup cheddar cheese,
  grated
½ teaspoon wholegrain mustard
8 large slices of country-style
  bread, lightly toasted
watercress salad, to serve

- Place the haddock in a shallow saucepan. Pour in the milk and simmer for 5–7 minutes, or until the fish flakes easily. Pour the milk through a strainer and reserve. Break the fish into large flakes, discarding the skin and any bones.

- Melt the butter in a separate saucepan. Stir in the flour and cook for 2 minutes. Slowly start to whisk in the ale, if using, followed by the reserved poaching milk until smooth. Bring to a boil, whisking, then simmer for a few minutes until thickened. Take off the heat and stir in the cheese, mustard, and haddock.

- Spread the mixture onto the toast, then cook under a preheated medium broiler for 3 minutes, or until golden and bubbling. Serve with a watercress salad.

10 Cheesy Smoked Mackerel Bites

Mix together a generous ¼ cup cream cheese, a smoked mackerel fillet, weighing about 5 oz skin (any bones discarded), and ¼ cup grated cheddar. Spread onto 4 pieces of toast, splash with a little Tabasco sauce, then cook under a medium broiler for 3–5 minutes, or until golden and bubbling.

30 Smoked Haddock Rarebit Bake

Heat 1 scant cup ale in a pan until boiling. Remove from the heat and stir in 2½ cups grated cheddar cheese until melted. Lightly beat 2 egg yolks in a bowl, then beat in 3 tablespoons of the ale and cheese mixture. Pour this back into the pan and cook over low heat for 3–5 minutes, or until the sauce starts to thicken. Add a few drops of Worcestershire sauce. Place 4 x 5 oz smoked haddock fillets into an oiled baking dish. Pour the sauce onto the fish and arrange a thinly sliced tomato on top. Place in a preheated oven at 425°F for 15 minutes, or until the top is golden and the fish is cooked through.

QuickCook
Midweek
Dinners

Recipes listed by cooking time

30

20

Baked Striped Mullet with Orange and Olive Couscous

Serves 4

4 striped mullet fillets, weighing about 5 oz each

¼ cup olive oil, plus extra for oiling

finely grated zest and juice of 1 orange, plus 1 whole orange

4 thyme sprigs

2 cups couscous

1¾ cups hot vegetable stock

finely grated zest and juice of ½ lemon

1 cup thinly sliced radishes

½ cup chopped pitted black olives

handful of flat-leaf parsley, chopped

salt and pepper

- Place the fish fillets on a lightly oiled baking pan. Season well with salt and pepper, then drizzle with 1 tablespoon of the oil and a little of the orange juice. Scatter with the thyme sprigs. Place in a preheated oven at 350°F for 15 minutes, or until just cooked.

- Meanwhile, place the couscous in a large bowl. Pour in the hot stock, cover, and leave for 5–10 minutes until all the liquid is absorbed and the couscous has swollen. Add the orange and lemon zest with a little more of the orange juice, the lemon juice, and the remaining oil, then leave to cool.

- Peel the remaining orange, discarding any white pith, then cut into small pieces and stir through with a fork, breaking up any clumps. Season and add the radishes, olives, and parsley just before serving with the fish.

---

10 Striped Mullet with Orange and Olive

Dressing Heat a ridged griddle pan until smoking hot. Brush 2 tablespoons olive oil over 4 x 4 oz striped mullet fillets and season well. Cook in the pan for 3–5 minutes until just cooked through. Toss together the finely grated zest of ½ orange, juice of ½ lemon, 3 tablespoons olive oil and ¼ cup chopped pitted black olives. Spoon the mixture onto the fish and serve.

30 Orange and Olive Baked Striped

Mullet Season 2 x 8 oz whole striped mullet, gutted and scaled, and place in a lightly oiled baking dish. Mix together 3 tablespoons olive oil, 1 tablespoon fresh lemon juice, and the juice of ½ orange. Cut the remaining ½ orange into slices and arrange around the fish along with 4 thyme sprigs. Pour the dressing onto the fish and place in a preheated oven at 350°F for 15 minutes. Scatter with ½ cup pitted black olives and bake for a further 5–10 minutes, or until the fish is cooked through. Serve one fillet per person.

FIS-MIDW-MOB

Tuna with Caramelized Onion and Sherry Sauce

Serves 4

3 tablespoons olive oil
2 onions, thinly sliced
2 garlic cloves, crushed
1 scant cup dry sherry
4 tuna steaks, weighing about
   6 oz each
salt and pepper
handful of flat-leaf parsley,
   chopped, to garnish

- Heat 2 tablespoons of the oil in a skillet. Add the onions and cook over low heat for 15–20 minutes, or until soft and starting to turn golden. Add the garlic and cook for 1 minute. Add the sherry and simmer for a few minutes until you have a rich sauce. Remove from the pan and set aside. Wipe the pan clean with paper towels.

- Heat the remaining oil in the pan. Season the tuna steaks well with salt and pepper, add the tuna to the pan, and cook for 1–2 minutes on each side until lightly browned. Pour the onion sauce over the tuna, scatter with the parsley, and serve immediately.

Tuna Salad with Sherry Dressing

Whisk together 1 tablespoon sherry vinegar and 3 tablespoons extra virgin olive oil until well blended, then season well with salt and pepper. Chop 1 roasted red pepper into strips. Toss with 4 cups arugula, 6 oz can of tuna, drained, and the dressing.

 Paprika Tuna with Sherry Dressing

Stir together 3 tablespoons olive oil, 1 tablespoon smoked paprika, the finely chopped leaves from 1 thyme sprig, and 1 crushed garlic clove, then season. Spread the mixture over 4 x 6 oz tuna steaks and leave to marinate for 10 minutes. Heat a ridged griddle pan until smoking hot. Brush away the excess marinade from the tuna and cook for 2 minutes on each side until golden on the outside but still rare inside. Whisk together 1 tablespoon sherry vinegar and 1½ tablespoons olive oil. Set the tuna on serving plates, drizzle with the dressing, and scatter with some chopped flat-leaf parsley to serve.

20 Shrimp Laksa

Serves 4

1 tablespoon vegetable oil

2 tablespoons laksa curry paste or Thai red curry paste mixed with a pinch of turmeric

1¾ cups chicken stock

13½ oz can coconut milk

1 lemon grass stick

1 fresh lime leaf

4 quails' eggs or 2 hens' eggs

4 oz dried medium rice noodles

½ lb raw large peeled shrimp

To serve

bean sprouts

cucumber matchsticks

cilantro, chopped

lime wedges

- Heat the oil in a large saucepan. Add the curry paste and cook for 2 minutes. Pour in the stock and coconut milk and add the lemon grass and lime leaf. Leave to simmer for 10 minutes.

- Meanwhile, cook the eggs in boiling water: 4 minutes for quails' eggs or 8 minutes for hens' eggs. Drain and cool under cold running water, then remove the shells and quarter or halve the eggs. Cook the noodles according to the package instructions.

- Remove the lemon grass and lime leaf from the curry. Add the shrimp to the pan and cook for 3 minutes, or until they turn pink and are cooked through, then drain the noodles and stir into the pan. Cook until heated through.

- Ladle into serving bowls. Arrange the eggs on top, then scatter with bean sprouts, cucumber matchsticks, cilantro, and lime wedges to serve.

---

10 Shrimp Cracker Bites

Heat 2 teaspoons vegetable oil in a nonstick skillet. Add 1 teaspoon laksa or Thai red curry paste and cook for 1 minute. Stir in 3½ oz cooked peeled small shrimp and heat through. Arrange on top of shrimp crackers and scatter with chopped cilantro and a little desiccated coconut to serve.

30 Shrimp and Sweet Potato Laksa

Wrap 2 teaspoons shrimp paste in foil. Cook in a dry skillet on high heat for 2 minutes on each side. Cool a little, then unwrap the foil and place the paste in a food processor with 1 shallot, 3 red chiles, 2 lemon grass sticks, 2 teaspoons minced fresh ginger root, 2 tablespoons macadamia nuts, and 2 teaspoons turmeric. Pulse until smooth. Heat

1 tablespoon vegetable oil in a saucepan. Cook the paste for 2 minutes. Add 1¾ cups each chicken stock and coconut milk. Simmer for 10 minutes. Add 2 peeled and cubed sweet potatoes and cook for 7 minutes. Add ½ lb raw peeled shrimp and cook for 3 minutes, or until they turn pink and are cooked through. Serve with a handful of bean sprouts and some cilantro leaves scattered on top.

Seafood Paella

Serves 4

1 tablespoon olive oil
3 oz chorizo, thickly sliced
1 onion, diced
1 red pepper, chopped
2 garlic cloves, minced
1½ cups paella rice
1 teaspoon smoked paprika
pinch of saffron threads
3½ cups hot chicken stock
10 oz cleaned live mussels
8 cooked king shrimp, shells on
3½ oz raw squid rings
½ cup frozen peas

- Heat the oil in a large, heavy saucepan. Add the chorizo and cook for about 2 minutes, or until starting to brown. Add the onion and pepper and cook for 3 minutes, then stir in the garlic and cook for another minute. Pour in the rice and stir until well coated.

- Add the paprika and saffron, return the chorizo to the pan, then pour in the hot stock. Bring to a boil, then simmer, uncovered, for 15 minutes. Add the mussels, cover the pan, and cook for 3 minutes. Stir in the shrimp, squid, and peas and cook for a further 2 minutes until the rice is tender (add a drizzle of hot water around the edge of the pan if still a little firm) and the mussels have opened—discard any that remain closed, then serve.

Saffron and Fennel Seafood

Heat 2 tablespoons olive oil in a large saucepan. Cook 1 diced fennel bulb for 2 minutes. Add ¾ cup dry white wine, a good pinch of saffron threads and 1 lb cleaned live mussels. Cover and cook for 3 minutes. Add 8 cooked peeled jumbo shrimp and 3½ oz raw squid rings. Cook for 2 minutes. Discard any mussels that remain closed before serving.

Paella-Style Seafood Pasta

Cook 3 oz sliced chorizo in 1 tablespoon olive oil in a large, heavy saucepan for 2 minutes. Remove. Add 1 diced onion. Cook for 5 minutes. Add 2 minced garlic cloves. Cook for 1 minute. Return the chorizo with 1 teaspoon smoked paprika to the pan and add ½ cup dry white wine. Boil for 2 minutes. Add 1¼ cups canned diced tomatoes and 3¾ cups vegetable stock.

Bring to a boil. Stir in 10 oz angel hair pasta broken into 1 inch pieces. Simmer for 7 minutes, stirring often, until nearly cooked through. Add 10 oz cleaned live mussels, cover, and cook for 3 minutes. Discard any that remain closed. Add 8 cooked peeled jumbo shrimp and 3½ oz raw squid rings. Cook for 2 minutes until the pasta is tender and the seafood is cooked through.

10 Cajun-Blackened Fish Steaks

Serves 4

3½ tablespoons butter, melted
4 sea bass fillets, weighing about
  6 oz each
2 tablespoons Cajun spice mix
2 teaspoons paprika
salt and pepper

To serve

lime wedges
green salad

- Brush plenty of the melted butter all over the fish fillets and season them well with salt and pepper. Mix the Cajun spice mix with the paprika and rub it all over the fish.

- Heat a large, dry skillet until smoking hot. Add the sea bass fillets and cook for 1–2 minutes. Turn them over and cook for a further 2–3 minutes, or until the fish is just cooked through and charred all over.

- Drizzle with any remaining butter and serve with lime wedges and a green salad.

20 Cajun Fish with Homemade Spice

Rub Mix together 1 tablespoon paprika, 1 teaspoon cayenne, ½ teaspoon each dried thyme and oregano, 2 crushed garlic cloves, and 2 tablespoons vegetable oil. Make a couple of slashes in the skin of 4 x 7 oz red snapper fillets. Rub the spice mix well into the fish and set aside for 5 minutes. Heat a ridged griddle pan until smoking hot and cook for 2–3 minutes on each side until charred and cooked through. Serve immediately.

30 Cajun Fish Stew

Melt 3 tablespoons butter in a saucepan over low heat. Stir in ¼ cup plus 1 tablespoon all-purpose flour and cook, stirring, for 10 minutes, or until dark brown. Add 2 teaspoons Cajun spice mix, then slowly whisk in 1¾ cups vegetable stock. Meanwhile, heat 1 tablespoon vegetable oil in a skillet and add 1 each diced onion, green pepper, and celery stick. Cook for 7 minutes, or until softened. Add them to the saucepan along with a 13½ oz can diced tomatoes, 1 bay leaf, and the leaves from 2 thyme sprigs. Leave to simmer for 10 minutes. Add a 10 oz skinless monkfish fillet, cut into medallions, and 3½ oz raw peeled shrimp and cook for 3–5 minutes until cooked through. Serve on plain cooked rice with plenty of Tabasco sauce.

3 ◑ Mackerel with Roasted Tomatoes and Horseradish

Serves 4

12 plum tomatoes, halved

3 tablespoons olive oil, plus extra for oiling

1 teaspoon superfine sugar

1 teaspoon red wine vinegar

4 mackerel fillets, weighing about 5 oz each

1¼ cups crème fraîche

1–2 tablespoons horseradish sauce

4 cups arugula

salt and pepper

- Place the tomatoes on a lightly oiled baking sheet. Drizzle with 2 tablespoons of the oil, then sprinkle each tomato half with a little sugar and vinegar. Place in a preheated oven at 400°F for 20–25 minutes, or until browned and soft.

- Meanwhile, heat a large, dry skillet until hot. Rub the remaining oil all over the mackerel and season well with salt and pepper. Add the mackerel to the pan, skin-side down, and cook for 5 minutes, or until the skin is golden. Turn the fish over and cook for a further 3 minutes, or until the fish is cooked through. Stir together the crème fraîche and horseradish sauce.

- Arrange the arugula, roasted tomatoes, and mackerel on serving plates and place with spoonfuls of horseradish sauce along the side.

 Mackerel and Sun-Dried Tomato Salad Gently toss together 3½ oz drained canned mackerel in olive oil, ½ cup drained sunblush tomatoes, and 3½ cups arugula. Whisk together the juice of ½ lemon, 3 tablespoons olive oil, and 1 tablespoon horseradish sauce. Drizzle onto the salad and serve.

 Baked Mackerel with Tomatoes Lightly oil 4 pieces of foil. Take 4 x 5 oz mackerel fillets and place one in the center of each piece of foil, then season with salt and pepper. Divide 2 sliced tomatoes, 1 minced shallot, and a handful of flat-leaf parsley among the fillets and place on top. Drizzle with more olive oil.

Fold the foil over tightly to seal, leaving a little air around the fish. Place on a baking pan in a preheated oven at 400°F for 15 minutes, or until cooked through. Stir 1 tablespoon horseradish sauce into 4 tablespoons mayonnaise and serve alongside.

Clams in Black Bean Sauce

Serves 4

2 tablespoons vegetable oil

2 scallions

2 garlic cloves, crushed

2 teaspoons minced fresh ginger root

1 red chile, minced

1 tablespoon black bean sauce

2 lb cleaned live clams

3 tablespoons chicken stock

1 tablespoon soy sauce

1 tablespoon Shaoxing wine

cilantro leaves, to garnish

- Heat the oil in a large saucepan over high heat. Meanwhile, slice the scallions and separate the white and green parts. Add the white part of the scallions, garlic, ginger, and chile to the pan and cook briefly until sizzling. Stir in the black bean sauce, then add the clams and remaining ingredients.

- Cover the pan and cook over medium heat for 3–5 minutes, or until the clams have opened. Discard any that remain closed. Divide onto serving plates and scatter with the green scallion and cilantro leaves to serve.

---

2 **Mussels in Black Bean Sauce**

Rinse 1 tablespoon fermented black beans. Mash with a little sugar. Briefly cook 2 sliced scallions, 2 crushed garlic cloves and 2 teaspoons each minced fresh ginger root and red chile in 2 tablespoons hot vegetable oil. Add the beans, 3 tablespoons chicken stock, and 2 tablespoons each soy sauce and Shaoxing wine. Bring to a boil, then simmer for 5 minutes. Meanwhile, heat 2 tablespoons oil in another pan. Cook 2 lb cleaned live mussels with 3 tablespoons hot water, covered, for 3–5 minutes, or until opened. Discard any that remain closed, along with the top shells. Drizzle with the sauce and serve.

3 **Sea Bass in Black Bean Sauce**

Place a 1¼ lb whole sea bass, gutted and scaled, in a heatproof dish. Pour over ¼ cup Shaoxing wine and add 1 tablespoon fresh ginger root, cut into matchsticks. Place in a steamer, cover, and cook for 15 minutes, or until cooked through. Pour off the poaching liquid and keep the fish warm. Heat 1 tablespoon vegetable oil in a skillet or wok over high heat. Stir-fry 2 crushed garlic cloves, 1 tablespoon minced fresh ginger root, and 2 diced scallions for a few seconds. Add ¼ lb ground pork and stir-fry for about 2 minutes until starting to turn golden. Pour in 1 scant cup chicken stock and 2 tablespoons each black bean sauce, soy sauce, and Shaoxing wine. Cook for about 5 minutes until the pork is cooked through. Mix 1 teaspoon cornstarch with 1 tablespoon water and add to the pan. Cook, stirring, until slightly thickened. Pour onto the fish and scatter with chopped cilantro to serve.

30 Leek and Smoked Haddock Risotto

Serves 4

13 oz smoked haddock fillet
3¾ cups hot vegetable stock
2 tablespoons butter
1 tablespoon vegetable oil
1 large leek, thickly sliced
1½ cups risotto rice
scant ½ cup dry white wine
½ cup mascarpone cheese
handful of chives, chopped,
   to garnish
salt

- Place the haddock in a shallow bowl. Pour the hot stock over the fish and leave for 5 minutes until nearly cooked through. Pour the stock through a strainer into a saucepan and keep hot. Break the fish into large flakes, discarding the skin and any bones.

- Meanwhile, heat the butter and oil in a large skillet over low heat. Add the leek and a splash of water, cover, and leave to gently cook for 7 minutes, stirring occasionally, until soft. Stir in the rice until well coated, then pour in the wine and cook for 2 minutes until nearly boiled off.

- Add the reserved hot stock, a ladleful at a time, stirring and simmering after each addition until the stock is absorbed before adding the next ladleful. After about 15 minutes when all the stock is absorbed and the rice is nearly cooked, add the fish and cook for a further 2 minutes, or until the rice is tender and still very moist. Stir in the mascarpone and season with salt. Cover and leave to stand for 2 minutes.

- Spoon into serving bowls and scatter with the chives.

 Leek-Crusted Haddock Fillets
Cook 1 large, very thinly sliced leek in boiling water for 4 minutes. Drain well. Meanwhile, cook 4 x 5 oz thin haddock fillets, skin-side up, under a preheated hot broiler for 3 minutes. Mix the leek with ¾ cup grated cheddar cheese. Turn the fish over, scatter with the leek mixture, and cook for a further 3–5 minutes, or until golden and bubbling and the fish is just cooked through.

 Smoked Haddock, Leek, and Potato Soup Heat 2 tablespoons butter with 1 tablespoon vegetable oil in a large saucepan. Add 1 large, thinly sliced leek and a splash of water, cover, and gently cook for 5 minutes, stirring every so often. Meanwhile, place 13 oz smoked haddock fillets in a shallow bowl. Pour over 3¾ cups hot vegetable stock. Leave for 5 minutes. Strain the stock into the pan. Add 1 peeled and diced potato. Simmer for about 12 minutes until the potato is soft, then mash slightly. Break the fish into large chunks, discarding the skin and any bones. Add to the pan with 1 scant cup milk. Heat through. Scatter with some chopped chives before serving.

10 Hake with Spicy Cilantro Pesto

Serves 4

¼ cup olive oil
4 hake steaks, weighing about
  6 oz each
2 green chiles
2 red chiles
4 cardamom seeds, ground
1 teaspoon caraway seeds, ground
1 garlic clove, crushed
bunch of cilantro
squeeze of lemon juice
salt and pepper

To serve

diced cucumber
pita bread

- Heat a ridged griddle pan until hot. Brush 1 tablespoon of the oil all over the fish steaks and season well with salt and pepper. Add the fish to the pan and cook for 3–5 minutes on each side, or until just cooked through.

- Meanwhile, place the remaining oil with all the other remaining ingredients in a small food processor and whiz until you have a smooth paste.

- Spoon the pesto over the fish and serve with a cucumber salad and pita bread.

---

20 Hake with Cilantro and Coconut Sauce

Heat 1 tablespoon vegetable oil in a saucepan. Cook 1 minced shallot for 5 minutes. Stir in 1 teaspoon minced fresh ginger root, 4 ground cardamom seeds and 1 minced red chile. Cook for 2 minutes. Pour over ½ cup coconut milk and 1 scant cup vegetable stock. Add 1 each fresh lime leaf and lemon grass stick, 1 tablespoon fish sauce, and ¼ teaspoon superfine sugar. Simmer for 10 minutes. Stir through a large handful of cilantro, chopped. Meanwhile, cook the hake fillets as above. Spoon the sauce onto the fish, discard the lime leaf and lemon grass, and serve.

30 Fish Soup with Cilantro Pesto

Heat 2 tablespoons vegetable oil in a saucepan. Cook 1 diced onion for 7 minutes until very soft. Add 2 crushed garlic cloves and 1 teaspoon minced fresh ginger root and cook for 2 minutes. Stir in 2 teaspoons ground cumin, 1 teaspoon ground coriander, and ½ teaspoon ground fennel. Pour in 3¼ pints (6¼ cups) water and bring to a boil. Add a rinsed and drained 15½ oz can chickpeas and simmer for 10 minutes. Scoop out and reserve a handful of chickpeas, then pulse the soup in a food processor until smooth. Return to the pan with the whole chickpeas and 2 x 6 oz skinless white fish fillets, such as hake. Cook for about 7 minutes until the fish flakes. Meanwhile, in a small food processor, pulse together the finely grated zest of 1 lime, 1–2 teaspoons fresh lime juice, 1 minced red chile, a large handful of cilantro, and 5–6 tablespoons vegetable oil. Drizzle the mixture over the soup and serve.

 # Lemon and Bacon-Wrapped Trout

Serves 4

4 small trout, gutted and scaled
2 lemons, thinly sliced
4 slices bacon
4 thyme sprigs
2 tablespoons olive oil, plus extra
    for oiling
salt and pepper

- Season the fish inside and out with salt and pepper and place on a lightly oiled baking pan. Place a couple of lemon slices in the cavity of each fish.

- Stretch the bacon with the back of a knife blade to thin it, then wrap a slice of bacon around each fish. Slip a thyme sprig under the bacon. Tuck any leftover lemon slices around the fish and drizzle with the oil.

- Place in a preheated oven at 425°F for 15–20 minutes, or until just cooked through. Serve immediately.

---

1 Open Lemon and Trout Sandwich

Stir together 4 tablespoons mayonnaise, the finely grated zest of ½ lemon, and a little of the juice. Mix in 2 x 3½ oz skinless smoked trout fillets. Lightly toast 4 slices of country bread. Spread the mayonnaise mixture onto the toast, set some cucumber slices and watercress sprigs on top, and serve.

 ### 3 Crispy Almond and Lemon Trout

Cut 3 thick slices of baguette into smaller, bite-size cubes. Mix together 1 crushed garlic clove, the finely grated zest of 1 lemon, and 5 tablespoons olive oil. Season 4 small gutted and scaled trout inside and out and place on a lightly oiled baking pan. Place a thyme sprig in the cavity of each fish along with a couple of lemon slices. Wrap a slice of bacon around each fish and tuck more lemon slices in around the fish. Scatter with the bread cubes and ¼ cup roughly chopped almonds, then drizzle with the flavored oil. Place in a preheated oven at 425°F for 15–20 minutes, or until just cooked through, and serve.

30 Spicy Peanut and Fish Stew

Serves 4

1 tablespoon vegetable oil

1 onion, diced

2 garlic cloves, crushed

1 teaspoon minced fresh ginger root

1 teaspoon ground coriander

pinch of freshly grated nutmeg

pinch of cayenne

13½ oz can diced tomatoes

¼ cup peanut butter

4 pollock or cod fillets, weighing about 6 oz each, skin on and cut into large chunks

squeeze of lime juice

To serve

¼ cup roasted peanuts, roughly chopped

cilantro

cooked plain rice

- Heat the oil in a large saucepan over medium heat. Add the onion and cook for 5 minutes, or until softened. Stir in the garlic and ginger and cook for 1 minute. Add the spices and cook for 1–2 minutes, then stir in the tomatoes and peanut butter. Add a little water and leave to simmer for 15 minutes.

- Add the fish to the pan and cook for a further 5 minutes, or until just cooked through. Season with salt and pepper, and add the lime juice, then serve scattered with chopped cilantro and peanuts and plain boiled rice.

 Spicy Peanut Fish Strips

Mix together 5 tablespoons peanut butter, 1 tablespoon soy sauce, and ¼ teaspoon superfine sugar. Cut ¾ lb skinless firm white fish fillets, such as cod, into strips. Brush with the peanut mixture, then drizzle with a little vegetable oil. Cook under a preheated hot broiler for 3 minutes on each side, or until just cooked through. Serve with lime wedges.

Fish in Peanut and Coconut Curry Sauce Heat 2 teaspoons vegetable oil in a saucepan. Cook 1 diced shallot for 3–5 minutes, or until softened. Stir in 1 tablespoon Thai red curry paste and 2 teaspoons minced fresh ginger root. Pour over ½ cup coconut milk, 1 scant cup hot vegetable stock, and 1 tablespoon fish sauce. Add 1 lemon grass stalk and 1 fresh lime leaf. Leave to simmer for 5–10 minutes, then stir in 3 tablespoons peanut butter. Meanwhile, heat 1 tablespoon vegetable oil in a large, nonstick skillet. Pat 4 x 5 oz skinless pollock or other white fish fillets dry with paper towels and season. Cook for 3–5 minutes on each side until just cooked through. Spoon the sauce all over the fish to serve.

Skate with Lemon Butter and Capers

Serves 2

¼ cup plus 1 tablespoon butter
4 skate wings, weighing about
8 oz each
juice of 1 lemon
3 tablespoons drained capers
salt and pepper

- Heat the butter in a large, nonstick skillet over low heat until melted and starting to turn brown. Season the skate wings with salt and pepper, and add to the pan along with the capers. Cook for 3 minutes on each side until lightly browned and just cooked through. Transfer the skate to serving plates and spoon the capers on top.

- Stir the lemon juice and capers through the butter in the pan, then drizzle over the skate and serve.

 Poached Skate with Black Butter

Place 2 x 8 oz skate wings in a large saucepan with ¼ cup dry white wine and 1 bay leaf. Pour in enough water to cover. Poach very gently for 10–15 minutes, or until just cooked through. Remove the skate and keep warm. Heat 3½ tablespoons butter in a small saucepan until it turns dark brown, watching carefully. Remove from the heat and stir in 3 tablespoons drained capers and a handful of flat-leaf parsley, chopped. Spoon the mixture onto the fish and serve with lemon wedges.

 Skate with Buttery Lemon Onions

Heat 2 tablespoons olive oil and 3 tablespoons butter in a skillet over low heat. Cook 1 sliced onion for 15 minutes, or until very soft. Add ¼ teaspoon sugar and cook for a further 5 minutes, or until well browned. Leave to cool a little, then stir in 2–3 teaspoons fresh lemon juice, the finely grated zest of ½ lemon, and a large handful of flat-leaf parsley, chopped. Meanwhile, heat 1 tablespoon olive oil in a large skillet over medium heat and add 2 x 8 oz skate wings. Cook for 3 minutes on each side until just cooked through. Serve with the onions.

Baked Sea Bream with Fennel

Serves 4

3 tablespoons olive oil, plus extra
    for oiling
4 small fennel bulbs, quartered
1 shallot, thinly sliced
1 garlic clove, sliced
4 sea bream, weighing about
    1¼ lb each, gutted and scaled
juice of ½ lemon
handful of oregano leaves
salt and pepper

- Heat 2 tablespoons of the oil in a saucepan and cook the fennel and shallot for 5 minutes, or until softened. Stir in the garlic and cook for a further 1 minute. Transfer the fennel mixture to a lightly oiled roasting pan and arrange the fish on top. Season with salt and pepper, then squeeze on the lemon juice and drizzle with the remaining oil. Scatter with a little of the oregano and cover with foil.

- Place in a preheated oven at 400°F for 10 minutes. Remove the foil and bake for a further 5–10 minutes, or until the fish is cooked through.

- Transfer to a serving plate, scatter with the remaining oregano, and serve.

1   Fennel Salad with Seared Sea Bream

Heat a ridged griddle pan until smoking hot. Rub 1 tablespoon olive oil over 4 x 6 oz sea bream fillets, then season with salt and pepper. Cook, skin-side down, for 5 minutes. Turn the fish over and cook for a further 3 minutes, or until cooked through. Meanwhile, use a very sharp knife to slice 1 large fennel bulb as thinly as you can. Toss with the juice of ½ lemon, 3 tablespoons olive oil, and a handful of flat-leaf parsley, chopped. Serve the fennel salad with the fish.

2   Broiled Whole Sea Bream

Using a sharp knife, make 3 shallow slashes across either side of 4 x 1¼ lb gutted and scaled sea bream. Mix together 1 teaspoon crushed fennel seeds, the finely grated zest of 1 lemon, and a handful of oregano leaves, chopped. Stir in 3 tablespoons olive oil. Rub this all over the fish inside and out. Cook on a hot barbecue or under a preheated hot broiler for about 8 minutes on each side, or until a little charred and cooked through. Squeeze the juice of 1 lemon all over the fish and serve.

 **Tuna Teriyaki with Wasabi Mashed Potatoes**

Serves 4

1½ lb potatoes, peeled and quartered

1 tablespoon vegetable oil

4 tuna steaks, weighing about 5 oz each

5 tablespoons soy sauce

2 tablespoons rice vinegar

2 tablespoons soft brown sugar

5 tablespoons crème fraîche

1 tablespoon wasabi paste

salt and pepper

steamed sugar snap peas, to serve (optional)

- Cook the potatoes in a saucepan of boiling water for 12–15 minutes, or until soft.

- Meanwhile, brush the oil all over the tuna steaks. Heat a ridged griddle pan until smoking hot. Add the tuna and cook for 2–3 minutes on each side for medium-rare. While the tuna is cooking, heat the soy sauce, vinegar, and sugar in a small saucepan for about 2 minutes until warmed and slightly syrupy. Mix together the crème fraîche and wasabi.

- Drain the potatoes and mash until smooth, then stir the wasabi mixture through them. Season well with salt and pepper. Spoon the mashed potatoes onto warmed serving plates along with the tuna. Drizzle with the warm sauce and serve with some steamed sugar snap peas, if you like.

 Tuna with Wasabi Butter

Mix together 3½ tablespoons softened butter and 2 teaspoons wasabi paste. Season 4 x 5 oz tuna steaks. Cook on a smoking hot ridged griddle pan for 2–3 minutes on each side for medium-rare. Place the butter on top before serving.

 Tuna Skewers with Wasabi Mayo

Mix together 5 tablespoons soy sauce and 2 tablespoons each rice vinegar and soft brown sugar until the sugar has dissolved. Cut 4 x 5 oz tuna steaks into bite-size pieces, pour over the soy sauce mixture, and leave to marinate for 20 minutes. Meanwhile, mix together a scant ½ cup mayonnaise and 1 tablespoon wasabi paste.

Place in a dipping bowl. Remove the tuna from the marinade and lightly pat dry with paper towels. Place some mixed white and black sesame seeds on a plate. Thread the tuna pieces onto metal skewers, then roll in the sesame seeds to coat. Drizzle with a little vegetable oil. Cook under a preheated hot broiler for about 2 minutes on each side until golden. Serve with the mayonnaise for dipping.

20 Monkfish, Chorizo, and Chickpea Stew

Serves 4

2 tablespoons olive oil

3½ oz chorizo, thickly sliced

3 garlic cloves, sliced

1 tablespoon tomato paste

¼ cup dry white wine

1¼ cups canned diced tomatoes

15½ oz can chickpeas, rinsed
   and drained

12 oz skinless monkfish fillet, cut
   into bite-size pieces

7 oz baby spinach

salt and pepper

- Heat the oil in a large saucepan. Add the chorizo and cook for about 2 minutes, or until starting to brown, then add the garlic and cook for 1 minute. Stir in the tomato paste and the wine and cook until nearly boiled off. Add the tomatoes and chickpeas and leave to simmer for 10 minutes, adding more water if necessary.

- Add the monkfish to the pan and cook for 5 minutes, or until just cooked through. Gently stir in the spinach and season, then serve.

 Chorizo Monkfish with Mashed Chickpeas Heat 1 tablespoon olive oil in a skillet. Cook 14½ oz skinless monkfish fillet, cut into bite-size pieces and seasoned, for 5 minutes, turning occasionally, until cooked through. Add 4 thin slices of chorizo for the last minute of cooking to make them crisp and brown. Meanwhile, boil 2 x 15½ oz cans chickpeas for 1 minute. Drain and mash with 3 tablespoons crème fraîche, 1–2 teaspoons lemon juice, and some chopped flat-leaf parsley. Serve with the fish, diced tomatoes, and lemon wedges.

 Chickpea Pancakes with Monkfish and Chorizo Beat together 1¼ cups chickpea (gram) flour, 1 cup water, and a good pinch of salt until smooth. Leave to rest for 15 minutes. Meanwhile, heat 2 tablespoons vegetable oil in a saucepan over medium heat. Add 1 sliced onion and 3½ oz thickly sliced chorizo and cook for 2 minutes. Add a 12 oz skinless monkfish fillet, cut into bite-size pieces, and cook for 3 minutes. Turn over, then add 2 sliced garlic cloves and ¾ cup halved cherry tomatoes and cook for about 2 minutes, or until the fish is cooked through and the tomatoes have wilted. Keep warm. Heat 1 teaspoon oil in a large, nonstick skillet over medium heat. Add a ladleful of the batter, swirl around the pan, and cook for 1–2 minutes. Turn over with a slotted turner and cook for 1 minute more. Keep warm between 2 plates and repeat with the remaining batter to make a further 3 pancakes. Spoon a little of the fish mixture onto the pancakes. Scatter with some cilantro leaves to serve.

30 Baked Sea Bass with Romesco Salad

Serves 3–4

3 lb whole sea bass, gutted and scaled

6 tablespoons olive oil

3 thyme sprigs

pinch of dried red pepper flakes

1 lemon, sliced

3 red peppers

¼ cup blanched almonds

3 tablespoons blanched hazelnuts

1 tablespoon sherry vinegar

1 crushed garlic clove

½ teaspoon smoked paprika

2 plum tomatoes, diced

handful of flat-leaf parsley, chopped

salt and pepper

- Using a sharp knife, make 3 shallow slashes across either side of the sea bass. Mix together 2 tablespoons of the oil, the thyme, and the chile and rub the mixture all over the fish. Place in a baking dish and arrange the lemon slices around. Bake in a preheated oven at 425°F for 20–25 minutes, or until just cooked through.

- Meanwhile, rub 1 tablespoon of the remaining oil over the peppers, place in a baking dish, and cook in the oven with the fish for 15–20 minutes, or until well browned. Transfer to a freezer bag and seal. After 5 minutes, peel off the skins, discard the cores and seeds, and chop.

- While the fish and peppers are cooking, heat a small, dry saucepan and cook the nuts for 3 minutes until lightly browned. Leave to cool a little, then roughly chop. Whisk together the vinegar, garlic, and paprika. Add the remaining oil and season well with salt and pepper. Toss with the peppers, tomatoes, nuts, and parsley. Serve the fish with the Romesco salad.

 Seafood Skewers with Romesco Sauce Heat a ridged griddle pan until hot. Thread 12 each of cooked peeled jumbo shrimp and cleaned scallops onto metal skewers. Drizzle with 1 tablespoon olive oil and cook on the pan for 3 minutes on each side until just cooked through. Meanwhile, in a small food processor, pulse together 2 roasted red peppers, ¼ cup toasted almonds, 3 tablespoons olive oil, 2 teaspoons sherry vinegar, and ½ teaspoon smoked paprika. Serve with the skewers for dipping.

 Romesco Seafood Stew Heat 3 tablespoons olive oil in a large saucepan. Add 1 diced onion and cook for 2 minutes. Stir in 2 sliced red peppers and cook for a further 5 minutes, or until softened. Stir in 2 crushed garlic cloves and the finely chopped leaves of 1 rosemary sprig. Add 1 teaspoon tomato paste and ½ teaspoon smoked paprika, followed by a scant ½ cup dry white wine. Boil for 1 minute until reduced, then add a 13½ oz can diced tomatoes. Bring to a boil, then simmer for 5 minutes. Add 1 lb cleaned live clams and ½ lb raw peeled jumbo shrimp and cook for 3 minutes. Stir in ½ cup toasted and roughly ground almonds. Cook for a further 2 minutes until thickened and the seafood is cooked through, discarding any clams that remain closed. Scatter everything with chopped flat-leaf parsley to serve.

Seared Sea Robin with Tapenade and Mashed White Beans

Serves 4

2 tablespoons olive oil
1 shallot, chopped
1 garlic clove, crushed
2 x 15 oz cans cannellini beans,
　rinsed and drained
¾ cup vegetable or chicken stock
4 sea robin fillets, weighing about
　5 oz each
salt and pepper

For the tapenade

2 oz can anchovy fillets in olive oil
1 crushed garlic clove
2 tablespoons drained capers
¾ cup pitted black olives
grated zest and juice of ½ lemon
large handful of flat-leaf parsley

- Heat 1 tablespoon of the oil in a saucepan. Add the shallot and cook for 5–7 minutes, or until softened. Stir in the garlic and cook for a further 1 minute. Add the beans and stock and leave to simmer for 5 minutes. Pulse in a food processor until smooth. Return to the pan and keep warm.

- Meanwhile, heat the remaining oil in a large, nonstick skillet. Season the sea robin with salt and pepper, add to the pan, skin-side down, and cook for 5 minutes until golden. Turn over and cook for a further 3–5 minutes until the fish is cooked through.

- While the fish is cooking, drain the oil from the anchovies and reserve. Roughly chop the anchovies with all the other tapenade ingredients and mix with the reserved anchovy oil until you have a coarse sauce.

- Place the mashed beans on a plate, place the fish on top, and then drizzle with the tapenade to serve.

 Seared Sea robin with Smashed Beans

Cook the sea robin as above. Meanwhile, boil 2 x rinsed and drained 15 oz cans cannellini beans for 2 minutes. Drain. Roughly mash with 4 tablespoons olive oil. Stir in ¼ cup chopped pitted black olives, 2 finely chopped anchovies, 1 thinly sliced scallion, and plenty of chopped flat-leaf parsley. Serve with the fish.

 Baked Beans with Seared Sea Robin

Cook 1 chopped shallot in 1 tablespoon olive oil for 5–7 minutes. Add 1 crushed garlic clove. Cook for 1 minute. Add 2 x rinsed and drained 15 oz cans cannellini beans and ¾ cup vegetable stock. Simmer for 5 minutes. Stir in 6 tablespoons crème fraîche. Spoon into a baking dish and cover with ½ cup dried bread crumbs. Place in a preheated oven at 400°F for 15 minutes. Meanwhile, cook the sea robin as above. While the fish is cooking, mix together ¾ cup pitted black olives, a generous 1¼ cups halved cherry tomatoes, 3 tablespoons olive oil, and 2 teaspoons each capers and red wine vinegar. Season with salt and pepper. Spoon the mixture onto the fish and serve with the beans.

1 Broiled Mullet with Yogurt Dill Sauce

Serves 4

4 striped mullet fillets, weighing
 about 5 oz each
2 tablespoons olive oil
5 tablespoons plain yogurt
juice of ½ lemon
2 garlic cloves, crushed
handful of dill, finely chopped
salt and pepper
chargrilled zucchini, to serve

- Season the fish fillets with salt and pepper, then rub them all over with 1 tablespoon of the oil. Cook on a ridged griddle pan over high heat for 5 minutes. Turn the fillets over and cook for a further 3–5 minutes, or until just cooked through.

- Meanwhile, mix together the remaining oil, yogurt, lemon juice, garlic, and dill, then season with salt and pepper.

- Spoon the sauce onto the fish and serve immediately with the chargrilled zucchini.

2 Striped Mullet with Tahini Yogurt

Sauce Heat 1 tablespoon olive oil and cook 1 small diced onion for 7 minutes, or until softened. Add 2 crushed garlic cloves and cook for 2 minutes. Stir in a handful of cilantro, chopped, and sizzle for a couple of seconds, then add a pinch of cayenne, the juice of ½ lemon and 3 tablespoons tahini paste. Stir until you have a smooth paste. Remove from the heat and slowly stir in 5 tablespoons plain yogurt. Cook the fish as above and serve with the sauce.

3 Indian Yogurt-Baked Haddock

Mix together 1¼ cups plain yogurt, 2 tablespoons ground coriander, 2 teaspoons ground cumin, 1 minced green chile and 1 teaspoon minced fresh ginger root. Place 4 x 6 oz thick haddock fillets in an oiled baking dish. Season the fish with salt and pepper, and pour in the yogurt mixture. Cut 3 tablespoons butter into small pieces and dot spoonfuls all over the fish. Cover with foil and place in a preheated oven at 375°F for 20 minutes, or until just cooked through. Transfer the fish to a serving plate. Stir a little more melted butter into the yogurt if it has split, then scatter with chopped cilantro and serve.

20 Halibut with Peas and Lettuce

Serves 4

3 tablespoons butter
2 tablespoons olive oil
2 shallots, diced
2 thick slices bacon diced into
 lardons
2 cups frozen peas
¾ cup hot chicken stock
5 tablespoons crème fraîche
2 Little Gem lettuces
4 halibut steaks, weighing about
 6 oz each
1–2 teaspoons fresh lemon juice
salt and pepper

- Heat 1 tablespoon of the butter and 1 tablespoon of the oil in a saucepan. Add the shallots and lardons and cook over low heat for 7–10 minutes, or until very soft. Stir in the peas and stock and simmer for about 5 minutes. Stir in the crème fraîche and season with salt and pepper. Roughly chop the lettuce and toss around the pan for 1 minute to coat in the juices.

- Meanwhile, heat the remaining oil in a skillet. Pat the fish dry with paper towels and season with salt. Cook for 5 minutes on each side, or until just cooked through. Add the remaining butter to the pan along with the fresh lemon juice and swirl around until the butter has melted.

- Serve the fish with the peas and lettuce together with some new potatoes, if liked.

10 Halibut with Pea and Mint Salad

Heat 1 tablespoon olive oil in a skillet. Pat 4 x 6 oz halibut steaks dry with paper towels and season with salt. Cook for 5 minutes on each side, or until just cooked through. Meanwhile, boil 2 cups frozen peas for 3 minutes. Drain and cool under cold running water. Whisk together 2–3 teaspoons fresh lemon juice and 3 tablespoons extra virgin olive oil. Season, and stir the mixture into the peas with a handful of mint leaves, chopped. Serve with the halibut.

30 Halibut Baked in Lettuce Leaves

Separate 8 large leaves from a romaine lettuce and trim off any thick stems. Place in a shallow dish, pour in some boiling water and leave for 2 minutes, or until softened. Drain and cool under cold running water. Remove any bones from 4 x 6 oz halibut steaks and season. Place each piece of fish on top of a lettuce leaf along with a handful of dill, then fold over to cover (add another leaf if it doesn't quite fit) and tuck the ends underneath. Heat 1 tablespoon butter and 1 tablespoon olive oil in an ovenproof skillet and cook the fish, seam-side down, for 1 minute. Pour in a scant ½ cup dry white wine and dot with a little more butter. Place in a preheated oven at 325°F for 15–20 minutes, or until just cooked through. Serve with boiled new potatoes and peas.

Pollock Wrapped in Parma Ham with Lentil Salad

Serves 4

1¾ cups dried Puy lentils
4 skinless pollock or cod fillets,
   weighing about 5 oz each
4 slices of Parma ham
5 tablespoons olive oil
2 tablespoons red wine vinegar
1 garlic clove, crushed
2 scallions, diced
3½ cups baby spinach
3 plum tomatoes, diced
salt and pepper

- Rinse the lentils, then drain, place in a saucepan, and cover with twice their volume of boiling water. Simmer for 15 minutes, or until just tender.

- Meanwhile, season the fish fillets with salt and pepper, then halve each slice of Parma ham and roughly wrap around each fillet. Heat a skillet, add 1 tablespoon of the oil, and cook the fish for 2 minutes, or until lightly browned on the underside. Drizzle another tablespoon of the oil onto the fish. Place the pan under a preheated hot broiler, making sure you turn the handle away from the heat if not flameproof, and cook for 5–7 minutes, or until just cooked through. Mix together the remaining oil, vinegar, and garlic.

- Cool the lentils a little under cold running water, then drain. Toss with the scallions, spinach, and tomatoes, then stir through the dressing. Serve alongside the fish.

 Shrimp, Lentil, and Parma Ham Salad

Drain and rinse 2 cups boiled lentils. Whisk together 3 tablespoons olive oil, 2 tablespoons red wine vinegar, and 1 crushed garlic clove and stir it through the lentils. Heat 2 teaspoons olive oil in a nonstick skillet and cook 4 slices of Parma ham for about 1 minute, or until just crisp. Toss 7 oz cooked peeled shrimp with the lentils, along with ½ cup drained sun-dried tomatoes in oil and 2 cups spinach leaves. Scatter with Parma ham to serve.

Lentil and Smoked Haddock Pilaf

Pour boiling water over a 13 oz smoked haddock fillet in a shallow saucepan to cover and gently cook for about 7 minutes, or until the fish flakes easily. Meanwhile, heat 1 tablespoon butter and 2 tablespoons vegetable oil in a skillet. Cook 1 diced onion for 5–7 minutes, or until soft. Stir in 2 crushed garlic cloves, 2 teaspoons minced fresh ginger root, and 1¾ cups basmati rice. Cook, stirring, for 1 minute, then add 1 teaspoon each ground cumin and coriander and ¼ teaspoon of turmeric. Lift out the fish, discard the skin and any bones, and break into large flakes. Fill the poaching water up to 4¼ cups and pour it over the rice mixture. Add a generous ½ cup rinsed and drained dried red lentils. Bring to a boil, then cover and cook for 15 minutes. Add ½ cup frozen peas and the fish. Cook for another 5 minutes until the peas and rice are tender. Scatter with chopped cilantro to serve.

Thai Green Curry with Monkfish and Tomatoes

Serves 4

2 tablespoons Thai green curry paste

handful cilantro

1 tablespoon vegetable oil

1¼ cups fish or chicken stock

13½ fl oz can coconut milk

2 tablespoons fish sauce

2 teaspoons soft brown sugar

1 lb skinless monkfish fillet, cut into 1 inch cubes

½ cup cherry tomatoes, halved

handful of basil, chopped, to garnish

- Put the Thai green curry paste and cilantro in a mini food processor and pulse to a smooth paste.

- Heat the oil in a large saucepan. Add the curry paste and stir around the pan for 3–5 minutes, or until the oil starts to separate. Pour in the stock and coconut milk and bring to a boil. Add the fish sauce and sugar and leave to simmer for 10 minutes.

- Stir in the monkfish and tomatoes and cook for a further 7–10 minutes, or until they are just cooked through. Scatter with the basil and serve.

 Monkfish with Green Curry Sauce

Cook 1 tablespoon Thai green curry paste in 1 tablespoon vegetable oil for 1–2 minutes. Add a scant ½ cup coconut milk, bring to a boil, then simmer. Meanwhile, cook 1 lb skinless monkfish fillet, cut into medallions ¾ inch thick and then seasoned, in 1 tablespoon vegetable oil in a large, nonstick skillet for 2–3 minutes on each side. Stir some chopped cilantro into the sauce. Pour the sauce over the fish to serve.

 Monkfish Thai Green Curry

Heat 2 tablespoons vegetable oil in a large saucepan. Add 2 tablespoons Thai green curry paste and cook for 3 minutes, or until the oil starts to separate. Pour in 1¼ cups fish or chicken stock, a 13½ fl oz can coconut milk, 2 tablespoons fish sauce, and 2 teaspoons soft brown sugar. Simmer for 10 minutes. Add 1½ cups trimmed green beans and cook for 1–2 minutes. Stir in 1 lb skinless monkfish fillet, cut into 1 inch cubes, and cook for 3–5 minutes. Scatter with a handful of basil leaves to serve.

FIS-MIDW-GYT

 # Peppered Tuna with Arugula and Parmesan

Serves 4

¼ cup plus 1 tablespoon extra virgin olive oil

13 oz very fresh tuna steak

1 tablespoon black peppercorns, coarsely crushed

1 tablespoon balsamic vinegar

3 cups wild arugula

salt

Parmesan cheese shavings, to serve

- Brush 1 tablespoon of the oil all over the tuna. Place the crushed peppercorns on a plate, then roll the tuna in the pepper until well coated. Wrap up tightly in a piece of foil. Heat a dry, heavy skillet until smoking hot. Place the wrapped tuna in the pan and cook for 7 minutes, turning every minute or so to cook evenly on each side. Remove from the pan and leave to cool a little.

- Whisk the remaining oil with the vinegar until well combined, then season with salt. Just before serving, unwrap the tuna and slice. Dress the arugula with the vinaigrette and arrange on serving plates. Arrange the tuna among the arugula and scatter with Parmesan shavings to serve.

 ### Arugula and Tuna Pasta Salad

Cook 11 oz quick-cook penne according to the package instructions. Drain and cool under the cold running water. Meanwhile, mix together 4 tablespoons mayonnaise, a 3 oz can of tuna, drained, and plenty of pepper. Stir into the pasta, then toss with 2 cups arugula to serve.

 ### Slow-Cooked Tuna with Arugula Pesto

Rub 1 tablespoon olive oil over 4 x 6 oz thick tuna steaks, place on a baking pan, and season well. Place in a preheated oven at 225°F for 25 minutes. Meanwhile, in a food processor, pulse together 3 cups arugula, 2 tablespoons grated Parmesan cheese, and 2–3 teaspoons fresh lemon juice. Stir in 5 tablespoons olive oil and 1 teaspoon drained capers. Drizzle the mixture onto the tuna to serve.

2⏱ Pad Thai

Serves 4

7 oz dried medium rice noodles

2 tablespoons vegetable oil

2 eggs, beaten

7 oz raw jumbo shrimp, tails on

2 garlic cloves, crushed

2 teaspoons tamazest paste (optional)

½ teaspoon dried red pepper flakes

2 tablespoons soft brown sugar

2 tablespoons fish sauce

3 scallions, sliced

½ cup bean sprouts

juice of ½ lime

2 tablespoons roasted peanuts, roughly chopped

cilantro, chopped, to garnish

- Cook the rice noodles according to the package instructions.

- Meanwhile, heat a large wok or skillet and add the oil. Add the eggs and leave to cook for 30 seconds, then stir and break up into small pieces. Add the shrimp, garlic, tamazest paste, if using, and dried red pepper flakes. Cook for a further 30 seconds, then add the sugar and fish sauce and cook for a couple of seconds longer.

- Drain the noodles well and stir into the pan along with the scallions and bean sprouts. Toss them around the in pan to heat through, then pour in the lime juice. Spoon onto serving plates and scatter with the peanuts. Scatter with the chopped cilantro to serve.

1⏱ Fast Pad Thai with Tofu

Heat 2 tablespoons vegetable oil in a large wok or skillet. Add 2 beaten eggs, then 2 crushed garlic cloves and ½ teaspoon dried red pepper flakes. Cook for 30 seconds, then stir to break up. Add 10 oz fresh egg noodles, 2 tablespoons each brown sugar and fish sauce, and a splash of water. Cook for 1 minute. Add ¾ cup bean sprouts, 5 oz each cubed tofu and cooked peeled shrimp and 1–2 teaspoons fresh lime juice. Heat through to serve.

3⏱ Pad Thai Rice Pot

Heat 2 tablespoons vegetable oil in a saucepan. Add 1 diced onion and cook for 5 minutes, or until softened. Add 2 teaspoons minced fresh ginger root and 2 crushed garlic cloves and cook for a further 1 minute. Stir in 1 generous tablespoon Thai green curry paste. Add 1½ cups jasmine rice, then pour in 3¼ cups vegetable or fish stock and 1 scant cup coconut milk. Season and bring to a boil, then leave to simmer for 15 minutes. Stir in 7 oz raw peeled jumbo shrimp and 1½ cups snow peas. Cook for 3–5 minutes, or until the shrimp turn pink and are cooked through. Squeeze the juice of ½ lime all over everything and scatter with plenty of chopped cilantro and some chopped roasted peanuts to serve.

20 Baked Plaice with Apple Cider and Mussel Sauce

Serves 4

2 tablespoons butter, plus extra for greasing

2 American plaice fillets, weighing about 7 oz each, halved

1 scant cup dry apple cider

1 shallot, diced

1 lb cleaned live mussels

¼ cup crème fraîche

handful of flat-leaf parsley, chopped

salt

- Rub a little butter over the inside of a baking dish, then place the fish fillets in the dish and season with salt. Dot all over with about half the butter, then pour in a couple of tablespoons of the apple cider. Cover loosely with a sheet of parchment paper, then place in a preheated oven at 350°F for 12–15 minutes, or until just cooked through.

- Meanwhile, heat the remaining butter in a large saucepan. Add the shallot and cook for 3–5 minutes, or until softened, then add the mussels and remaining cider. Cover the pan and cook for 5 minutes, or until the mussels have opened. Discard any that remain closed. Stir in the crème fraîche and parsley.

- Place the fish on serving plates and spoon the mussels and sauce on top to serve.

 Smoked Trout and Apple Cider Salad

Stir together ½ cup mascarpone cheese, 1 tablespoon apple cider vinegar, 1–2 tablespoons horseradish sauce and a handful of dill, chopped. Break 2 x 3½ oz skinless smoked trout fillets into large flakes, discarding any bones. Cut 2 apples into thin slices. Arrange on serving plates with 3½ cups watercress, then drizzle with the dressing.

 Baked Plaice with Cider Lentils

Heat 1 tablespoon butter and 1 tablespoon olive oil in a saucepan. Add 1 diced shallot and cook for 3–5 minutes until softened. Add 2 thin slices Canadian bacon and 1 crushed garlic clove and cook for a further 2 minutes, or until lightly browned. Add a scant ½ cup rinsed and drained dried Puy lentils and pour in 1 scant cup apple cider. Bring to a boil, then simmer for 15–20 minutes, or until just tender, adding extra water if necessary. Meanwhile, bake the American plaice fillets as above. Spoon the lentils onto a plate and set the plaice fillets on top. Add a spoonful of crème fraîche mixed with chopped flat-leaf parsley to each portion to serve.

QuickCook
Healthy

Recipes listed by cooking time

10

Steamed Sea Bream with Asian Flavors

Serves 2

½ inch piece of fresh ginger root
2 lemon grass stalks, diced
1 garlic clove, sliced
½ red chile, minced
1 fresh lime leaf, finely sliced
handful of cilantro, chopped
3 tablespoons fish sauce
1 tablespoon vegetable oil, plus
   extra for oiling
2 sea bream fillets, weighing
   about 5 oz each
plain rice, to serve

- Peel the ginger and cut into matchsticks. Mix with the lemon grass, garlic, chile, lime leaf, cilantro, fish sauce, and oil.

- Place each fish fillet on a lightly oiled piece of foil, skin-side down and pour the dressing onto it. Fold the foil over tightly to seal, leaving a little air around the fish.

- Place the foil packages in a steamer set over simmering water. Cook for 10–15 minutes, or until the fish is just cooked through. Serve with plain rice.

Mussels with Asian Flavors

Heat 1 tablespoon vegetable oil in a large saucepan over medium heat. Add 2 minced lemon grass stalks, ½ inch piece of fresh ginger root, peeled and cut into matchsticks, 1 sliced garlic clove, and ½ red chile, minced, and cook for 30 seconds. Add 3 tablespoons fish sauce, ¼ cup coconut milk, and 1 lb cleaned live mussels. Cover and cook for about 5 minutes, or until the mussels have opened. Discard any that remain closed. Toss in 10 oz fresh rice noodles and heat through. Scatter generously with chopped cilantro to serve.

Fish Rice with Asian Flavors

Heat 2 teaspoons vegetable oil in a saucepan over low heat. Add 1 crushed garlic clove, ½ green chile, minced, and 1 teaspoon grated fresh ginger root. Cook gently for 1 minute to soften. Add 1 minced lemon grass stalk and 1½ cups brown long-grain rice. Pour in 2½ cups water and season. Cover and simmer for 20 minutes, placing 2 x 5 oz sea bream fillets on top of the rice for the last 5 minutes of cooking. Remove from the heat and leave to steam for about 8 minutes, or until the rice and fish are just cooked through. Scatter with chopped cilantro and serve.

Tuna Burgers with Mango Salsa

Serves 4

1 large mango, seeded, peeled, and sliced

¼ red onion, thinly sliced

2 tablespoons olive oil

juice of ½ lime

½ red chile, minced

handful of cilantro, finely chopped

1 lb tuna steak, cut into large chunks

½ shallot, diced

1 tablespoon soy sauce

4 whole-wheat hamburger buns, split open

salt and pepper

- Toss together the mango, onion, 1 tablespoon of the oil, lime juice, chile, and cilantro and set aside.

- Place the tuna in a food processor with the shallot and soy sauce. Briefly pulse until the mixture just comes together but isn't pureed. Lightly wet your hands, then shape into 4 burgers.

- Heat a ridged griddle pan until smoking hot. Season the tuna burgers with salt and pepper, and brush them all over with the remaining oil. Cook the burgers on the pan for 1–2 minutes on each side, or until browned but still rare inside. Toast the hamburger buns, then place a spoonful of mango salsa inside. Place the burgers on top of the salsa and serve.

Tuna Strips in Pita Breads

Cut 1 lb tuna into thin strips. Heat a ridged griddle pan until smoking hot. Toss the tuna in a little olive oil. Cook on the pan on one side only for 1 minute. Toss with 1 tablespoon chopped red onion, ½ chopped mango, and a handful of cilantro leaves. Divide the mixture between 4 toasted pita bread pockets, add a dollop of sour cream to each, if you like, and serve with lime wedges.

Tuna Steak Burgers with

Teriyaki Onions Rub a little olive oil all over 4 x 5 oz tuna steaks and place on a baking pan. Place in a preheated oven at 225°F for 20–25 minutes until cooked rare to medium. Meanwhile, heat 1 tablespoon olive oil in a skillet. Add 1 sliced onion and cook over low heat for 20 minutes, or until soft and caramelized. Add 2 tablespoons soy sauce, 1 tablespoon mirin, and 2 teaspoons superfine sugar. Cook for a further 5 minutes until the liquid has evaporated. Place each tuna steak into a split hamburger bun and place the onions on top.

3 Broiled Striped Mullet with Mediterranean Vegetable Sauce

Serves 4

¼ cup olive oil
1 onion, diced
2 garlic cloves, crushed
13½ oz can diced tomatoes
handful of basil, chopped
1 red pepper, quartered
1 small eggplant, thickly sliced
1 zucchini, thickly sliced
4 striped mullet fillets, weighing
  about 5 oz each
salt and pepper

- Heat 1 tablespoon of the oil in a saucepan. Add the onion and cook over low heat for 7 minutes, or until softened. Add the garlic and cook for 1 minute. Stir in the tomatoes and basil and leave to simmer for 10 minutes.

- Meanwhile, rub 2 tablespoons of the oil all over the vegetables and season well with salt and pepper. Heat a griddle pan until smoking hot and cook the vegetables in batches for 3–5 minutes on each side, or until lightly charred. Add to the tomato sauce to gently cook.

- Brush the remaining oil all over the fish fillets and season. Set the griddle pan, skin-side down, and cook for 5–7 minutes, or until browned and crisp. Turn the fillets over and cook for a further 3 minutes until just cooked through.

- Season the sauce and spoon onto serving plates. Place the fish fillets on top and serve.

 Mediterranean Vegetable Shrimp Pasta Roughly chop 1 each roasted red pepper and roasted eggplant from a jar. Stir into 1¼ cups ready-made spicy tomato pasta sauce and heat through. Add 7 oz cooked peeled jumbo shrimp and heat through. Meanwhile, cook 1 lb fresh linguine according to the package instructions. Drain and toss with the sauce in the pan. Scatter with chopped basil to serve.

 Red Snapper with Mediterranean Vegetables To make a red pepper coulis, rub a little olive oil all over 1 red pepper. Place under a preheated hot broiler for about 10 minutes and cook until blackened. Seal in a freezer bag for 5 minutes then peel off the skin and discard the core and seeds. In a food processor, roughly pulse with 1 tablespoon olive oil, 1 teaspoon white wine vinegar, and a handful of basil leaves. Thinly slice 2 zucchini with a vegetable peeler. Season and drizzle with olive oil. While you are preparing the coulis and zucchini, heat a ridged griddle pan until smoking hot. Brush 1 tablespoon olive oil all over 2 x 12 oz red snapper fillets and season. Set the fish on the pan, skin-side down, and cook for 5–7 minutes, or until browned and crisp. Turn the fish over and cook for 3 minutes more, or until just cooked through. Serve with the coulis spooned on top and the zucchini on the side.

1 Tuna Soba Noodles with Ponzu Dressing

Serves 2

7 oz dried soba noodles
1 tablespoon vegetable oil
2 tuna steaks, weighing about 4 oz each
¼ cucumber, sliced
2 scallions, sliced
2 tablespoons soy sauce
2 tablespoons mirin
juice of ½ lime
2 teaspoons superfine sugar
salt and pepper
sesame seeds, to serve

- Cook the noodles according to the package instructions. Meanwhile, heat a ridged griddle pan until smoking hot. Rub the oil all over the tuna steaks and season well with salt and pepper. Cook in the pan for 1–2 minutes on each side, or until charred on the outside but still rare inside.

- Drain the noodles, cool under cold running water, and drain again, then divide between serving bowls.

- Cut the tuna into slices and toss together with the cucumber and scallions. Mix together the soy sauce, mirin, lime juice, and sugar until the sugar has dissolved. Pour the sauce onto the noodles and scatter with sesame seeds to serve.

2 Sesame Tuna with Noodles

Cook 7 oz dried udon noodles according to the package instructions and drain. Heat 1 tablespoon vegetable oil in a wok. Add 2 sliced scallions and 1 sliced garlic clove and stir-fry briefly. Add 1 cup halved shiitake mushrooms and 1 cup sugar snap peas. Stir-fry for 2 minutes. Add 2 tablespoons each soy sauce and mirin, a pinch of superfine sugar, and the noodles. Cook for 2 minutes. Meanwhile, press 3 tablespoons sesame seeds all over 2 x 4 oz tuna steaks. Cook on a smoking hot griddle pan for 1–2 minutes on each side, then serve immediately.

3 Tuna and Soba Noodles in Broth

Place 3 large strips of konbu in a saucepan and cover with 4½ cups cold water. Leave to soak for 15 minutes. Bring very slowly to a boil. Just before boiling point, remove the konbu. Add a handful of bonito flakes and simmer for 3 minutes, or until they sink. Strain, reserving the liquid. Cook 7 oz dried soba noodles according to the package instructions. Meanwhile, rub 1 tablespoon vegetable oil all over 2 x 4 oz tuna steaks and season well. Cook on a smoking hot ridged griddle pan for 1–2 minutes on each side. Use a vegetable peeler to slice ½ thin cucumber into strips. Divide the noodles between 2 serving bowls, pour in the broth and place the tuna and cucumber strips on top.

20 Plaice with Beans and Chorizo

Serves 4

2 tablespoons olive oil

1 onion, diced

2 garlic cloves, minced

2 x 15 oz cans fava beans, rinsed and drained

¾ cup vegetable stock

1 strip of orange zest

1 bay leaf

4 American plaice fillets, weighing about 5 oz each

8 thin slices of chorizo

salt and pepper

handful of flat-leaf parsley, chopped, to garnish

- Heat 1 tablespoon of the oil in a saucepan. Add the onion and garlic and cook for 5 minutes, or until softened. Add the beans, stock, orange zest, and bay leaf and leave to simmer for 10 minutes until soft and most of the liquid has boiled off. Season well with salt and pepper.

- Brush the remaining oil all over the fish fillets. Cook under a preheated hot broiler for 3–5 minutes on each side, or until the fish flakes easily. Meanwhile, place the chorizo in a dry, nonstick skillet and cook for 1 minute on each side until brown and crisp.

- Remove the bay leaf and orange zest from the beans, then spoon onto serving plates, place the fish and chorizo on top, and scatter with the parsley.

---

10 Plaice with Chorizo and Mashed Beans

Place 2 thin slices of chorizo on top of 4 x 5 oz American plaice fillets and cook under a preheated hot broiler for 3–5 minutes on each side, or until the fish flakes easily. Meanwhile, place 2 x 15 oz cans fava beans, rinsed and drained, in a saucepan, pour in enough boiling water to cover, and cook for 1 minute. Drain and mash together with 4 tablespoons milk. Serve alongside the fish.

30 Plaice with Chorizo Cassoulet

Heat 1 tablespoon olive oil in a saucepan. Add 1 diced onion, 2 minced garlic cloves, and 2 oz chopped chorizo and cook for 5 minutes. Add 2 x 15 oz cans fava beans, rinsed and drained, ¼ cup vegetable stock, and ¼ cup milk. Simmer for 5 minutes. Stir ¼ cup low-fat crème fraîche through the mixture and it pour into a baking dish. Cover evenly with

½ cup dried bread crumbs mixed with the finely chopped leaves from 1 thyme sprig. Place in a preheated oven at 375°F for 10–15 minutes until bubbling and browned Meanwhile, brush 1 tablespoon olive oil all over 4 x 5 oz American plaice fillets. Cook under a preheated hot broiler for 3–5 minutes on each side, or until the fish flakes easily. Serve with the bean mixture.

30 Healthy Fish Supper with Homemade Tomato Ketchup

Serves 4

1½ lb potatoes, scrubbed and cut into french fries

3 tablespoons olive oil

½ onion, sliced

1 teaspoon finely grated fresh ginger root

1 garlic clove, crushed

½ teaspoon ground coriander

1 tablespoon tomato paste

1½ cups cherry tomatoes

¼ cup white wine vinegar

2 tablespoons soft brown sugar

2 tablespoons low-fat mayonnaise

4 skinless cod loins, weighing about 5 oz each

¾ cup dried whole-wheat bread crumbs

finely grated zest of 1 lemon

salt and pepper

- Cook the french fries in boiling water for 3 minutes, or until just starting to soften. Drain and pat dry with paper towels. Toss with 2 tablespoons of the oil, season with salt and pepper, and place on a large baking pan. Place in a preheated oven at 425°F for 25 minutes, or until golden and cooked through.

- Meanwhile, heat the remaining oil in a saucepan over medium heat. Add the onion and cook for 10 minutes, or until softened. Add the ginger, garlic, coriander, and tomato paste and cook for a further 2 minutes. Add the tomatoes, vinegar, sugar, and a splash of water. Leave to simmer for 10 minutes. Pulse in a small food processor or blender to form a chunky ketchup. Season and set aside.

- While the ketchup is simmering, spread the mayonnaise all over the cod loins. Combine the bread crumbs and lemon zest in a bowl. Dip the fish in the bread crumb mixture until coated all over. Place on a cookie sheet and cook in the oven, with the fries, for 12 minutes, or until just cooked through. Serve the fish with the fries and ketchup.

---

10 Crunchy Tomato Fish Bites

Cut 4 x 5 oz skinless cod loins into bite-size pieces and toss with 2 tablespoons red pesto. Coat with ¾ cup dried whole-wheat bread crumbs. Set on a baking pan and drizzle with olive oil. Bake in a preheated oven at 425°F for 7 minutes, or until cooked. Serve with potato salad.

20 Sea Bass with Tomato Pesto Pasta

In a food processor, pulse together a large handful of basil, 1 crushed garlic clove, ¼ cup grated Parmesan cheese and 2 tablespoons olive oil. Cook 13 oz dried linguine according to the package instructions. Meanwhile, heat 2 teaspoons olive oil in a nonstick skillet over medium heat. Cut 2 x 5 oz sea bass fillets into pieces and cook in the skillet, skin-side down, for 3 minutes. Turn the fish over and cook for 3 minutes more. Drain the pasta. Add the pesto to the pasta and toss to coat. Then add ¾ cup halved cherry tomatoes and the fish, (first discarding the skin, if liked), toss to combine, and serve.

Sea Bream with Tomatoes and Basil

Serves 4

3 tablespoons olive oil

2 sea bream, weighing about
  1 lb each, gutted and scaled

3 garlic cloves, sliced

1 cup cherry tomatoes, halved

1 red chile, sliced

¼ cup dry white wine

1 scant cup water

handful of basil leaves, torn

salt and pepper

- Heat the oil in a large skillet over medium heat. Season the fish with salt and pepper, then add to the pan with the garlic, tomatoes, and chile and cook for 1–2 minutes. Add the wine and measurement water and cook for 7 minutes. Carefully turn and for another 7 minutes, or until just cooked through. Transfer the fish to a warmed serving dish.

- Cook the sauce over high heat for 30 seconds to reduce a little. Stir the basil into the sauce and then pour it over the fish. Allow 1 fillet per person and serve with crusty bread and a green salad.

Thai-Style Fish with Tomatoes and Basil

Heat 1 tablespoon olive oil in a large, nonstick skillet. Add 1 minced garlic clove and 1 teaspoon minced fresh ginger root. Cook for 30 seconds. Add ½ lb skinless fish fillets, cut into chunks, and cook for 3 minutes. Add ¾ cup cherry tomatoes and cook for 3 minutes. Mix 1 tablespoon fish sauce with 1 teaspoon superfine sugar and stir into the skillet. Cook for a further 1–2 minutes. Add a handful of chopped basil and serve.

Baked Sea Bream with Tomatoes and Basil

Lightly oil 2 sheets of foil. Peel and slice 2 potatoes very thinly. Lay the slices in the center of each piece of foil. Set 2 small gutted and scaled sea bream on top of each. Divide ½ cup diced tomatoes between the fish cavities along with a handful of basil leaves. Scatter ½ cup diced tomatoes on top of the fish along with 2 teaspoons drained capers and a little olive oil. Season with salt and pepper. Fold the foil over tightly to seal, leaving a little air around the fish, and place on a baking pan. Place in a preheated oven at 425°F for 20–25 minutes, or until the fish and potatoes are cooked through. Serve 1 fillet per person.

30 Smoked Salmon Sushi Salad

Serves 4

1¼ cups sushi rice, well rinsed and very well drained

2 cups water

7 tablespoons rice vinegar

2 tablespoons superfine sugar, plus an extra pinch

2 tablespoons sesame seeds

3 tablespoons soy sauce

2 teaspoons finely grated fresh ginger root

1 avocado, stoned, peeled, and sliced

7 oz smoked salmon slices

2 scallions, sliced

2 tablespoons toasted, thinly sliced nori sheets, to garnish

salt

- Place the rice in a saucepan, pour in the measurement water, and season with salt. Bring to a boil, then cook for 10–12 minutes, or until most of the water has boiled off and small craters appear in the surface of the rice. Cover with a tightly fitting lid, remove from the heat, and leave to steam for 5 minutes. Meanwhile, combine 4 tablespoons of the vinegar and the 2 tablespoons sugar until the sugar has dissolved.

- Pour the rice onto a baking pan. Pour over the vinegar mixture and use a spatula to stir through in a slicing motion until the rice looks glossy. Cover with damp paper towels and leave to cool a little.

- Cook the sesame seeds in a small dry, skillet over low heat until lightly browned.

- Mix together the remaining vinegar, soy sauce, ginger, and the pinch of sugar. Spoon the rice into serving bowls. Arrange the avocado, smoked salmon, and scallions on top. Drizzle with the dressing. Cut the toasted nori into thin strips and scatter them over everything along with the sesame seeds.

 Smoked Salmon Rice Crackers

Arrange 8 rice crackers on a plate. Place 1 small chopped avocado and 3½ oz smoked salmon strips on top. Drizzle with 1½ tablespoons each rice vinegar and soy sauce mixed with 1 teaspoon finely grated fresh ginger root and ¼ teaspoon of sugar. Scatter with 1 sliced scallion to serve.

 Stir-Fried Salmon with Noodles

Heat 1 tablespoon vegetable oil in a nonstick wok or skillet. Cut 2 x 4 oz skinless salmon fillets into chunks, add to the pan and stir-fry for 5–7 minutes, or until just cooked then remove. Add 1 sliced onion to the pan and stir-fry until softened. Add 1 crushed garlic clove and 1 teaspoon finely grated fresh ginger root and continue to stir-fry for 30 seconds. Toss in 10 oz fresh rice noodles. Pour in 3 tablespoons soy sauce and 1 tablespoon mirin and cook for 1–2 minutes. Return the salmon to the pan with 3½ cups watercress, cook until wilted, and serve.

 # Tomato and Fennel Fish Pie

Serves 4

¼ cup olive oil

1 fennel bulb, chopped

2 garlic cloves, sliced

1¼ cups cherry tomatoes

1 tablespoon tomato paste

¼ cup dry white wine

1 scant cup water

10 oz skinless cod fillets, cut into chunks

5 oz raw peeled jumbo shrimp

1½ lb potatoes, peeled and cut into chunks

2 scallions, sliced

salt and pepper

- Heat 1 tablespoon of the oil in a saucepan. Add the fennel and garlic and cook for 5–7 minutes, or until softened. Add the tomatoes and tomato paste and cook for a further 2 minutes until softened. Pour in the wine and cook until nearly boiled off, then add the measurement water and fish. Cook for 3 minutes. Add the shrimp and cook for 3–5 minutes, or until just cooked through.

- Meanwhile, cook the potatoes in a saucepan of salted boiling water for 12–15 minutes, or until soft. Drain and mash the potatoes with the remaining oil, the scallions, and a little water to loosen. Season well with salt and pepper.

- Arrange the fish and sauce in a baking dish. Spoon the mashed potatoes on top. Place under a preheated hot broiler and cook for 3 minutes, or until browned. Serve immediately.

 Shrimp with Tomato and Fennel Mayo Arrange 11 oz cooked peeled jumbo shrimp on a plate. Whisk together 3 tablespoons mayonnaise, 3 tablespoons fromage frais, 2 finely chopped sun-dried tomatoes, 1 teaspoon crushed fennel seeds, and 1–2 teaspoons fresh lemon juice. Serve with the shrimp, a crisp green salad, and some crusty brown bread.

 Cod with a Tomato, Fennel, and Potato Crust Place 4 x 6 oz cod fillets on a lightly oiled baking pan. Season, then place 2 thinly sliced tomatoes on top. Scatter with 1 crushed garlic clove and ½ teaspoon coarsely ground fennel seeds. Use a mandoline or food processor to slice 2 peeled potatoes very thinly. Arrange the potato slices on top of the tomatoes and lightly brush with olive oil. Place in a preheated oven at 375°F for 20 minutes, or until the fish is cooked through and the potatoes are crisp.

Halibut Ceviche with Grapefruit and Chiles

Serves 2

14½ oz skinless halibut fillet
2 limes
1 grapefruit
¾ cup cherry tomatoes, halved
1 red chile, seeded (optional) and sliced
handful of mint, finely chopped
1 tablespoon extra virgin olive oil
salt and pepper

- Using a very sharp knife, cut the fish into thin slices.

- Grate the zest from 1 lime into a medium-sized bowl, then squeeze in the juice from both limes. Cut the base off of the grapefruit, then cut around the flesh to remove the zest and pith. Slice into segments and set aside. Add any juice from the grapefruit to the bowl. Add the fish to the lime and grapefruit juices and toss to coat. Leave to marinate for 15 minutes.

- Discard the marinade from the fish. Arrange the fish on a serving plate with the grapefruit segments and tomatoes. Scatter with the chile and mint, season with salt and pepper, and drizzle with the oil to serve.

---

10 Spicy Halibut and Grapefruit Salad

Mix together 1 tablespoon vegetable oil, ½ red chile, minced, and a handful of cilantro, finely chopped. Toss with 14½ oz skinless halibut fillet, cut into bite-size pieces. Cook under a preheated hot broiler for 2–3 minutes on each side. Meanwhile, peel 3 segments of grapefruit and cut into small pieces. Whisk 1 tablespoon vegetable oil with 1 tablespoon rice vinegar and toss it with 3½ cups mixed salad leaves and another handful of cilantro leaves. Arrange the grapefruit and halibut on top, and serve.

30 Halibut with Grapefruit Quinoa

Salad Place 1¾ cups quinoa in a saucepan. Add 2 cups water and season with salt. Bring to a boil, cover with a tight-fitting lid, and simmer for 15 minutes. Remove from the heat and leave to cool for 1 minute. Meanwhile, rub a little olive oil all over 1 red pepper. Place under a preheated hot broiler and cook for about 10 minutes, or until blackened all over. Seal in a freezer bag for 5 minutes. Working over a bowl to catch the juices, cut off the base of a grapefruit, then cut around to remove the zest. Slice 1 half into segments and squeeze the juice from the other half. Mix the grapefruit juice with ½ teaspoon grated fresh ginger root, 1 teaspoon clear honey, and 1 tablespoon olive oil. Stir this through the quinoa. Peel the pepper, discard the core and seeds, and chop. Add to the quinoa with 2 sliced scallions, the grapefruit segments, and a handful of cilantro leaves. Rub a little vegetable oil all over 14½ oz skinless halibut fillet. Place under the broiler and cook for 4–5 minutes on each side, or until cooked through. Serve with the salad.

FIS-HEAL-HAQ

1 Lemon and Tomato Swordfish Kebabs

Serves 4

11½ oz swordfish, cut into
  1¼ inch chunks
1 tablespoon olive oil
1 lemon, sliced
handful of fresh bay leaves
12 cherry tomatoes
salt and pepper
mixed green salad, to serve

- Toss the fish in the oil to coat, then season with salt and pepper. Chop the lemon slices in half.

- Heat a ridged griddle pan until smoking hot. Thread the fish chunks onto metal skewers, alternating with the lemon slices, bay leaves, and tomatoes.

- Cook the kebabs on the griddle pan over high heat for 4 minutes on each side, or until the fish is cooked through. Serve with a mixed green salad.

 Swordfish Steaks with Orange and Tomato Sauce Heat 1 tablespoon olive oil in a large skillet over medium heat. Add 2 minced garlic cloves and cook for 30 seconds. Pour over a 13½ oz can diced tomatoes and 2 strips of orange zest. Leave to simmer for 5 minutes. Add 4 x 6 oz swordfish steaks, cover, and leave to simmer for 12 minutes, until just cooked through. Stir in a handful of pitted green or black olives and serve with some crusty bread.

 Lemony Swordfish with Tomato Sauce Place 4 x 6 oz swordfish steaks on a plate, cover with a mixture of 1 tablespoon olive oil, the juice and finely grated zest of 1 lemon, and a handful of oregano, chopped. Set aside to marinate. Meanwhile, heat 1 tablespoon olive oil in a skillet over medium heat. Add 2 red peppers, quartered, 1 teaspoon superfine sugar, and 1 tablespoon white wine vinegar and let it cook gently for 10 minutes. Add 1¼ cups cherry tomatoes. Cook for a further 10–15 minutes, or until the vegetables are very soft. Season well with salt and pepper. While the vegetables finish cooking, place the swordfish under a preheated hot broiler and cook for 7 minutes on each side. Serve with the peppers and tomatoes.

20 Oven-Baked Thai Fishcakes

Serves 4

1 lb skinless firm white fish fillets
2 tablespoons fish sauce
1 tablespoon Thai red curry paste
1 teaspoon superfine sugar
¾ cup green beans, thinly sliced
handful of cilantro, chopped
2 teaspoons vegetable oil
salt and pepper

To serve

sweet chili sauce
cucumber wedges

- Place the fish, fish sauce, curry paste, and sugar in a food processor and pulse until smooth. Stir through the green beans and cilantro, then season with salt and pepper.

- Brush a 12-hole muffin pan with the oil, then spoon 2–3 tablespoons of the mixture inside each hole, lightly pressing down the mixture. Place in a preheated oven at 400°F for 12–15 minutes, or until golden and cooked through. Serve with sweet chili sauce and cucumber wedges.

---

10 Thai Fish Salad

Cut 10 oz skinless firm white fish fillets into large chunks. Cover with boiling water and simmer for 3–5 minutes until cooked through then drain. In a large bowl mix 1 minced red chile, 2 tablespoons fish sauce, 1 tablespoon superfine sugar, and the juice of 1 lime together. Stir in 3 oz cooked peeled jumbo shrimp and the fish. Add 6 cups crisp salad leaves and toss to coat. Scatter with 2 tablespoons chopped roasted peanuts.

30 Thai Salmon Cakes with Dipping Sauce

In a food processor, pulse together 1 lb skinless salmon fillet, 1 egg white, 2 tablespoons fish sauce, 1 tablespoon Thai green curry paste, and 1 tablespoon superfine sugar until smooth. Mix in 1 finely chopped fresh lime leaf and a handful of cilantro, chopped. Shape into 12 patties. Chill for 5–10 minutes to firm up. Heat 2 tablespoons vegetable oil in a skillet. Cook the fishcakes for 5–7 minutes on each side, or until golden and cooked through. Meanwhile, make a dipping sauce by heating together 3 tablespoons white wine vinegar, 2 tablespoons superfine sugar, and ¼ cup water in a saucepan until the sugar has dissolved. Keep cooking until the mixture turns syrupy. Leave to cool. Stir in 1 tablespoon diced cucumber, 1 minced red chile, and 2 teaspoons fish sauce. Serve with the fishcakes.

30 Cod in Tomato and Olive Sauce

Serves 4

1 tablespoon olive oil

1 onion, sliced

2 garlic cloves, minced

1 tablespoon tomato paste

13½ oz can diced tomatoes

¼ teaspoon sugar

handful of thyme leaves

4 skinless cod fillets, weighing
  about 4 oz each

¼ cup pitted black olives

salt and pepper

new potatoes, to serve (optional)

- Heat the oil in a large, deep skillet. Add the onion and cook for 5 minutes, or until softened, then add the garlic and cook for a further 2 minutes. Stir in the tomato paste and cook for 1 minute, then pour in the tomatoes. Add the sugar and thyme and season with salt and pepper, then reduce the heat and leave to simmer for 10 minutes.

- Slide the fish fillets into the sauce along with the olives, cover loosely with kitchen foil, and leave to simmer for 8–10 minutes, or until the fish flakes easily. Serve with some boiled new potatoes, if you like.

 Cod with Tapenade and Tomatoes
Spread 4 teaspoons tapenade all over 4 x 4 oz thin cod fillets. Thinly slice 1 tomato and set 1 slice on top of each piece of fish. Drizzle with a little olive oil. Place under a preheated hot broiler and cook for 7–10 minutes, or until the fish is just cooked through.

 Olive-Crusted Cod with Tomato Salad
Finely chop ¼ cup pitted black olives and mix with ½ cup dried bread crumbs and a handful of chopped flat-leaf parsley. Rub 1 tablespoon olive oil all over 4 x 7 oz cod fillets, place on a baking pan, and press the bread crumb mixture on top. Place in a preheated oven at 400°F for 15 minutes, or until the fish is cooked through. Five minutes before the end of cooking, whisk together 1 tablespoon olive oil, 1 teaspoon white wine vinegar, and ¼ teaspoon of sugar. Toss with 1¼ cups cherry tomatoes and a large handful of basil leaves. Serve with the fish.

 Smoked Trout, Cucumber, and Radish Salad

Serves 2

2 tablespoons mayonnaise

2 tablespoons fromage frais

lemon juice, to taste

4 oz skinless smoked trout fillets,
  broken into large flakes

½ cucumber, sliced

6 radishes, thinly sliced

2 cups watercress

pepper

toasted country-style bread,
  to serve

- Mix together the mayonnaise and fromage frais with lemon juice to taste and season well with pepper.

- Arrange the trout, cucumber, radishes, and watercress on a serving plates. Drizzle the mayonnaise mixture on top and serve with plenty of toasted country-style bread.

 Trout with Radish and Cucumber Tzatziki Rub olive oil all over 2 x 4 oz trout, gutted and scaled, and season. Place a lemon slice in each fish cavity, then cook on a hot barbecue or under a preheated hot broiler for 7 minutes on each side, or until the fish flakes easily. Meanwhile, finely chop ¼ cucumber and thinly slice 3 radishes. Mix with 1 small crushed garlic clove, a generous ¼ cup plain yogurt, and some finely chopped dill. Serve alongside the trout.

 Trout, Pickled Cucumber, and Radish Salad Thinly slice ½ cucumber and mix with 1 tablespoon each superfine sugar and rice vinegar, and ¼ teaspoon of salt. Leave to stand for 25 minutes until lightly pickled. Drain and toss together with 6 thinly sliced radishes and a handful of flat-leaf parsley, chopped. Serve the salad with 4 oz smoked trout fillets, kept whole, and some steamed new potatoes.

30 Coconut Fish Curry

Serves 4

1 tablespoon vegetable oil
½ teaspoon mustard seeds
1 teaspoon cumin seeds
10 curry leaves
1 onion, chopped
1 tablespoon minced fresh
   ginger root
1 garlic clove, minced
1 red chile, minced
1 teaspoon ground coriander
½ teaspoon turmeric
1 scant cup water
1 tablespoon tamazest puree
4 halibut steaks, weighing about
   6 oz each
3 tomatoes, diced
½ scant cup low-fat coconut milk
salt and pepper
plain boiled rice, to serve

- Heat the oil in a large dry skillet over high heat. Add the seeds and cook for a few seconds until they start to pop, then add the curry leaves and cook for another few seconds until they turn golden. Reduce the heat, add the onion, ginger, garlic, and chile and cook over a medium heat for 5 minutes until softened.

- Add the coriander and turmeric and cook for 30 seconds. Stir in the measurement water and tamazest and leave to simmer for 5 minutes. Add the fish and tomatoes, cover, and gently cook for about 5 minutes, or until the fish is just cooked through. Pour in the coconut milk and heat through. Season with salt and pepper, and serve with plain boiled rice.

 Curried Coconut Fish Fingers

Cut 4 x 6 oz halibut steaks into long, thin slices. Rub 1 tablespoon curry paste all over the fish slices, then press ½ cup desiccated coconut into the steaks to coat. Drizzle with a little vegetable oil. Cook under a hot broiler for 3 minutes. Turn the fish over and cook for a further 3 minutes and serve.

 Griddled Fish with Coconut Rice

Place 1½ cups white long-grain rice in a saucepan. Pour in 1 scant cup coconut milk and 1¾ cups water and season with salt. Bring to a boil, cover, and simmer for 15 minutes, or until the rice is just tender. Meanwhile, mix together ½ red chile, minced, a handful of cilantro leaves, chopped, and 2 teaspoons vegetable oil. Toss with 4 x 6 oz halibut steaks and season with salt and pepper. Heat a ridged griddle pan until smoking hot. Cook the fish for 5 minutes on each side, or until just cooked through. Serve with the rice.

 # Broiled Sea Bass with Salsa Verde

Serves 4

olive oil, for oiling

4 sea bass fillets, weighing about
   5 oz each

salt and pepper

For the salsa verde

3 tablespoons olive oil

large handful of flat-leaf parsley

small handful of basil

1 garlic clove, crushed

juice of ½ lemon

1 tablespoon drained capers

To serve

boiled new potatoes

green salad

- Rub a little olive oil all over the fish fillets and season. Heat a ridged griddle pan until smoking hot. Griddle the fish, skin-side down, for 7 minutes, or until the skin is crisp and golden. Turn over the fish over and cook for a further 5 minutes until just cooked through.

- Meanwhile, pulse together the salsa verde ingredients in a small food processor until you have a rough paste.

- Place the fish on serving plates and spoon over the salsa verde. Serve with boiled new potatoes and a green salad.

 Spaghetti with Salsa Verde and Tuna

Prepare the salsa verde as above, then stir in a 6 oz can of tuna, drained. Meanwhile, cook 1 lb fresh spaghetti according to the package instructions. Drain the pasta, return it to the pan, and stir in the tuna and salsa verde. Serve immediately.

 Sea Bass Stuffed with Salsa Verde

Prepare the salsa verde as above. Divide 2 sea bass, weighing about 2½ lb each, gutted and scaled, into fillets and season with salt and pepper. Thinly slice 1 lemon and arrange half the slices down the center of a lightly oiled baking pan. Cover them with 2 fish fillets, skin-side down. Spread the salsa verde all over the fish, then set the other fillets on top and cover with the remaining lemon slices. Cook in a preheated oven at 450°F for 15–20 minutes, or until just cooked through. Place on a warm serving platter and serve with boiled new potatoes and a green salad.

Oatmeal Herrings with Beet Salad

Serves 4

scant ½ cup all-purpose flour

1 egg, beaten

1¼ cups medium or coarse oatmeal

4 boned and butterflied herrings, weighing about 6 oz each

3 tablespoons vegetable oil

½ shallot, minced

1 tablespoon sherry vinegar

3 tablespoons extra virgin olive oil

6 oz ready-cooked fresh beets, thinly sliced

3½ cups watercress

1 orange, peeled and segmented

salt and pepper

- Place the flour, egg, and oatmeal on separate plates. Season the herrings with salt and pepper, then dip into the flour until coated all over. Place the flesh side only into the egg. Let any excess egg drip off, then press the flesh side into the oatmeal to coat.

- Heat the oil in a large, nonstick skillet. Cook the herrings, oatmeal-side down, for 3–5 minutes, or until browned. Turn the fish over carefully and cook for a further 3 minutes to crisp the skin.

- Whisk together the diced shallot, vinegar, and oil, then season well with salt and pepper. Toss the mixture with the beets, watercress, and orange. Arrange on serving plates with the herring.

Kipper Salad with Oatmeal Topping

Cook ¼ cup oatmeal gently in a dry skillet for 3–5 minutes, or until golden. Season and let cool. Whisk together ½ minced shallot, 1 tablespoon sherry vinegar, and 3 tablespoons extra virgin olive oil. Season well with salt and pepper. Toss with 7 oz skinless kipper fillets, torn into chunks, 6 oz thinly sliced ready-cooked fresh beets, 3½ cups watercress, and 1 peeled and segmented orange. Sprinkle with the oatmeal, then serve.

Oatmeal Kipper Cakes with Beet Salad

Cook 2 peeled and chopped potatoes in a saucepan of lightly salted boiling water for 12–15 minutes, or until soft. Drain, then roughly mash and mix with 10 oz skinless kipper fillets. Use your hands to form the mixture into 4–6 large fishcakes. Place a scant ½ cup all-purpose flour, 1 beaten egg, and 1¼ cups medium or coarse oatmeal on separate plates. Dip the fishcakes into the flour, then into the egg, and finally press into the oatmeal until coated. Heat 3 tablespoons vegetable oil in a large, nonstick skillet. Cook the fishcakes for 3–5 minutes on each side, or until golden all over. Meanwhile, prepare the beet salad as above. Serve the fishcakes with the salad.

 # Baked Tuna with Italian Topping

Serves 4

4 tuna steaks, weighing about
  5 oz each
2 tablespoons olive oil, plus
  extra for oiling
¾ cup diced tomatoes
½ cup pitted black olives, roughly
  chopped
1 teaspoon drained capers
1 teaspoon red wine vinegar
handful of basil, chopped
salt and pepper

- Season the tuna steaks well, then brush all over with 1 tablespoon of the oil. Mix the remaining oil with the remaining ingredients.

- Place the tuna steaks on a lightly oiled baking pan and place the tomato mixture on top. Cook in a preheated oven at 425°F for 12–15 minutes until the fish is opaque and the tomatoes are lightly charred. Serve immediately with a green salad.

 ### Seared Tuna with Fresh Tomato Salad

Rub 2 teaspoons olive oil allover 4 x 3½ oz thin tuna steaks and season. Heat a ridged griddle pan until smoking hot and cook the tuna for 2 minutes on each side until brown on the outside but still rare on the inside. Meanwhile, toss together 1 cup diced tomatoes, 2 teaspoons balsamic vinegar, and 1 tablespoon extra virgin olive oil. Stir in a handful of basil, chopped. Spoon the tomato mixture onto the cooked fish to serve.

 ### Tuna with Puttanesca Sauce

Heat 1 tablespoon olive oil in a large skillet over medium heat. Add 4 anchovy fillets in oil, drained, and cook until they dissolve into the oil. Add 1 minced onion and cook for 4 minutes until softened, then 2 sliced garlic cloves and cook for a further 1 minute. Stir in 2 teaspoons tomato paste. Pour in a 13½ oz can diced tomatoes. Leave to simmer for 15 minutes, adding extra water if necessary. Add 4 x 5 oz tuna steaks to the pan along with 1 teaspoon drained capers and ½ cup pitted black olives. Simmer for 4 minutes then turn the tuna over and cook for a further 4 minutes until cooked through. Scatter with basil leaves before serving.

1 Roasted Salmon with Peach Salsa

Serves 4

1½ tablespoons olive oil

4 salmon steaks, weighing about
    5 oz each

2 peaches, stoned and chopped

½ teaspoon finely grated fresh
    ginger root

juice of ½ lime

1 tablespoon diced red onion

½ green chile, sliced

handful of basil, chopped

salt and pepper

- Rub ½ teaspoon of the oil all over the salmon steaks and season well with salt and pepper. Cook under a preheated hot broiler for 5 minutes. Turn the salmon over and cook for a further 3–5 minutes until just cooked through.

- Meanwhile, combine the remaining oil with the remaining ingredients and spoon the mixture on top of the salmon to serve.

2 Barbecued Salmon with Peach Sauce

Roughly chop 2 peaches. Place in a saucepan with 5 tablespoons tomato ketchup, 1 tablespoon apple cider vinegar, 1 tablespoon soft brown sugar, 1–2 teaspoons fresh lime juice, and a pinch of dried red pepper flakes. Simmer for 10 minutes. Pulse in a food processor until smooth. Lightly oil 4 x 5 oz salmon fillets and brush all over with the sauce. Cook on a hot barbecue, skin-side down, for 5 minutes. Turn over, brush with any remaining sauce, and cook for 3 minutes more, then serve.

3 Peach and Ginger Baked Salmon

In a food processor, roughly pulse together 2 stoned peaches, 1 teaspoon minced fresh ginger root, 1 tablespoon rice vinegar, and a handful of basil leaves until you have a chunky sauce. Place a 1¼ lb whole salmon fillet on a lightly oiled baking pan. Pour the peach sauce on top, season with salt and pepper, and drizzle with olive oil. Roast in a preheated oven at 400°F for 20 minutes, or until just cooked through.

30 Couscous and White Fish Parcels

Serves 4

1¼ cups hot vegetable stock
scant ½ cup frozen fava beans
½ cup frozen peas
1 generous cup couscous
2 scallions, sliced
4 sea bass fillets, weighing about
   5 oz each, skin on
1 lemon, sliced
1 tablespoon extra virgin olive oil
¼ cup plain yogurt
handful of dill, chopped
salt and pepper

- Bring the stock to a boil in a saucepan, add the beans, and cook for 1 minute. Add the peas and cook for a further 2 minutes. Pour the stock and vegetables over the couscous in a heatproof bowl. Cover and leave to stand for 7–10 minutes until the couscous has swollen. Stir through the scallions with a fork.

- Divide the couscous between 4 large sheets of parchment paper set on a large baking pan. Place a fish fillet on top of each, place a few lemon slices on top of each, drizzle with the oil, and season with salt and pepper. Fold the paper over tightly to seal, leaving a little air around the fish.

- Place in a preheated oven at 400°F for 15 minutes until the parcels puff a little. Meanwhile, mix together the yogurt and dill. Open the parcels at the table and spoon over the yogurt.

---

10 One-Pot Couscous

Cook 1 cup frozen peas in 1¼ cups boiling vegetable stock for 2 minutes. Meanwhile, heat 1 tablespoon olive oil in a large skillet over medium heat. Add 4 x 5 oz skinless sea bass fillets, cut into chunks, and fry for 1 minute. Add 2 sliced garlic cloves and cook for a further minute. Stir in 1 generous cup couscous and the stock and peas. Cover and leave to stand for 7 minutes. Stir in 1 sliced scallion and some chopped dill. Drizzle with plain yogurt and serve.

20 Couscous Bites with Mashed Peas

Place 1 generous cup couscous in a heatproof bowl. Add 1¼ cups hot vegetable stock, cover, and leave to stand for 7 minutes to swell. Stir in a handful of dill, chopped. Cut 4 x 5 oz skinless sea bass fillets into chunks. Dust 2 tablespoons all-purpose flour over the fish, then dip the fish in 1 beaten egg. Add the fish to the couscous and coat all over. Heat 1 tablespoon olive oil in a nonstick pan over medium heat. Add the fish and cook for 3–4 minutes on each side.

Meanwhile, cook 1¼ cups frozen peas in a saucepan of lightly salted boiling water for 3 minutes until tender. Drain and pulse in a food processor with 1 chopped scallion and 2 tablespoons plain yogurt. Serve alongside the fish.

20 Asian Fishball Soup

Serves 4

3¼ pints (6¼ cups) light fish or
  chicken stock
¾ inch piece of fresh ginger
  root, peeled
2 garlic cloves, peeled
1 red chile, halved
¼ cup Shaoxing wine or dry sherry
10 oz skinless haddock fillet,
  cubed
1 egg white
¼ cup rice flour
1 tablespoon soy sauce
2 heads bok choy, sliced
5 oz dried medium egg noodles
1 generous cup canned bamboo
  shoots, drained
2 scallions, sliced

- Heat the stock in a large saucepan. Add the ginger, garlic, 1 chile half, and the Shaoxing wine or sherry and simmer while you make the fishballs.

- Place the fish, egg white, rice flour, and soy sauce in a food processor and pulse until really smooth. Lightly wet your hands, then shape into walnut-size balls.

- Remove the ginger, garlic, and chile from the stock. Add the fishballs and cook for 3 minutes.

- Add the bok choy to the stock and simmer for 5 minutes. Meanwhile, cook the noodles according to the package instructions. Drain, then stir into the soup along with the bamboo shoots and heat through.

- Ladle into serving bowls and scatter with the remaining chile, minced, and the scallions.

---

10 Stir-Fried Fish with Greens

Heat 1 tablespoon vegetable oil in a wok or large skillet. Cut 10 oz skinless white fish fillet into large pieces. Dust with a little cornstarch. Cook, stirring often, for 1–2 minutes. Add 2 heads sliced bok choy and 1½ cups halved shiitake mushrooms. Cook for a further 3 minutes until the fish is cooked through. Stir in 2 tablespoons each soy sauce and rice wine and heat through. Serve with rice noodles.

30 Asian Fishballs in Fresh Broth

Heat 1 tablespoon vegetable oil in a saucepan. Add 1 diced shallot and cook for 2 minutes, or until softened. Add 2 peeled garlic cloves, a ¾ inch piece of fresh ginger root, peeled, and the bones from 3 fish. Cook for a further 3 minutes. Pour in 4¼ pints (8½ cups) light fish or chicken stock and leave to simmer for 15 minutes. Meanwhile, make the fishballs as above. Strain the stock into a clean saucepan. Add the fishballs and cook for 3 minutes. Add 2 sliced heads bok choy and simmer for 3 minutes, then stir in 5 oz fresh rice noodles and 1 generous cup drained canned bamboo shoots. Cook for a further 2 minutes, or until the bok choy is tender and the noodles and bamboo shoots are heated through, then serve.

 # Shrimp and Fennel Salad with Basil Citrus Dressing

Serves 2

½ orange
½ lime
½ small shallot, chopped
1 cup basil leaves
¼ cup extra virgin olive oil
1 fennel bulb, thinly sliced
3½ oz bag mixed salad leaves
5 oz cooked peeled jumbo shrimp
salt and pepper

- Squeeze the juice of the orange and lime into a small food processor, add the shallot and basil, and pulse briefly. With the motor running, slowly add the oil in a thin stream to make an emulsified, smooth dressing, then season with salt and pepper.

- Arrange the remaining ingredients on serving plates. Drizzle with the dressing and serve.

 ### Shrimp, Mussels, and Fennel with

Basil Sauce Heat 1 tablespoon olive oil in a saucepan. Add 1 each diced shallot and fennel bulb and cook for 5 minutes until softened. Add 1 crushed garlic clove and 3 skinned, seeded, and diced tomatoes. Cook for 2–3 minutes. Add a scant ½ cup water, 3 oz raw peeled jumbo shrimp, and 7 oz cleaned live mussels. Cover and cook for about 5 minutes, or until the mussels have opened and the shrimp are cooked through. Discard any mussels that remain closed. Pulse together a large handful of basil, ¼ cup olive oil, and 1–2 teaspoons fresh lemon juice in a small food processor. Drizzle the seafood with the mixture and serve.

 ### Creamy Fennel and Shrimp Risotto

Heat 2 tablespoons olive oil in a deep skillet. Add 1 minced onion and 1 diced fennel bulb and cook for 5 minutes, or until softened. Stir in ¾ cup risotto rice until well coated. Add the finely grated zest of ½ lemon. Pour in ¼ cup dry vermouth and cook until nearly boiled off. Add about 1¼ cups hot vegetable stock, a ladleful at a time, stirring and simmering after each addition until the stock is absorbed before adding the next ladleful. Continue until all the stock is absorbed and the rice is tender, about 15 minutes. Stir through 3½ oz cooked peeled jumbo shrimp and leave to stand for 2 minutes before serving.

30 Spiced Fish Tagine

Serves 4

3 garlic cloves, peeled
1 teaspoon ground cumin
1 teaspoon ground paprika
pinch of turmeric
juice of 1 lemon
large handful of cilantro, chopped
handful of flat-leaf parsley,
   chopped
2 tablespoons olive oil
2 halibut steaks, weighing about
   7½ oz each
½ lb new potatoes, halved
1 green pepper, sliced
1½ cups cherry tomatoes, halved
¾ cup pitted black olives
scant ½ cup water
salt and pepper

- Use a mortar and pestle to crush 2 of the garlic cloves and pound together with the spices, lemon juice, most of the cilantro, the parsley, and 1 tablespoon of the oil until you have a paste. Alternatively, use a small food processor. Rub most of the paste all over the halibut steaks, season with salt and pepper, and leave to marinate.

- Cook the potatoes in a saucepan of lightly salted boiling water for 10 minutes, then drain. Meanwhile, place a saucepan over medium heat, add the remaining oil and garlic clove, sliced, and cook for a couple of seconds. Add the green pepper and cook for 2 minutes. Stir in the tomatoes, olives, and reserved spice paste and cook until the tomatoes start to soften.

- Place the potatoes in a tagine or deep skillet with a lid. Scatter with half the tomato mixture, then add the fish. Spoon the remaining tomato mixture on top, then drizzle with the measurement water. Cover and cook for 10–15 minutes, or until the fish is cooked through. Serve with couscous or crusty bread.

---

10 Spiced Fish Pitas

Pound together 2 crushed garlic cloves, 1 teaspoon each ground cumin and paprika, the juice of 1 lemon, a handful each of cilantro and parsley, chopped, and 1 tablespoon olive oil. Smear this all over 4 x 5 oz tilapia fillets. Cook under a preheated hot broiler for 2½ minutes each side. Serve in toasted pita bread with salad.

20 One-Pot Spiced Fish Couscous

Cook 1 thinly sliced onion, 1 chopped garlic clove, and 2 teaspoons minced fresh ginger root in 1 tablespoon olive oil in a deep skillet over medium heat for about 5 minutes, or until soft and starting to brown. Meanwhile, make the spice paste (see left). Stir around the pan. Add 4 x 6 oz halibut steaks. Cook for 2 minutes on each side. Stir in 2 cups couscous and 1 cup halved cherry tomatoes. Pour 1¾ cups hot vegetable stock. Stir once. Cover and leave to stand for 5–8 minutes, or until the fish is cooked through. Stir in 2 tablespoons extra virgin olive oil and a handful of cilantro, chopped, before serving.

 **20** # Broiled Mackerel with Lemon, Chile, and Cilantro

Serves 4

grated zest and juice of 1 lemon
1 green chile, minced
handful of cilantro, chopped,
 plus extra to garnish
1 tablespoon vegetable oil,
 plus extra for oiling
4 medium mackerel, scaled
 and gutted
salt and pepper

- Mix together the lemon zest and juice, chile, cilantro, and oil. Using a sharp knife, make 3 shallow slashes across either side of each fish. Season with salt and pepper, and rub all over with the lemon mixture.

- Place the fish in a lightly oiled broiler pan and cook under a preheated hot broiler for about 7 minutes. Turn the fish over and cook for a further 5 minutes, or until the fish is just cooked through. Scatter with chopped cilantro and serve with lemon wedges, chapatis, and a tomato salad.

---

 1 ### Spiced Smoked Mackerel Pâté

Mash 2 x 5 oz skinless smoked mackerel fillets with a fork or in a food processor. Stir in ¼ cup plus 1 tablespoon low-fat cream cheese, then add 1–2 teaspoons fresh lemon juice, ½ green chile, minced, and a handful of cilantro, chopped. Serve with naan bread and a green salad.

 3 ### Mackerel in a Rich Curry Sauce

Heat 1 tablespoon vegetable oil in a saucepan over medium heat. Add 1 thinly sliced onion and cook for about 8 minutes, or until soft and golden. Stir in 2 minced garlic cloves and 2 teaspoons minced fresh ginger root. Cook for 30 seconds, then add 2 teaspoons each ground cumin and coriander and ½ teaspoon turmeric. Pour in 2 x 13½ oz cans diced tomatoes and simmer for 10 minutes. Meanwhile, cut 3½ oz skin-on mackerel fillets into large chunks. Add to the curry along with a large handful of cilantro, chopped. Simmer for 7–10 minutes, or until the fish is cooked through. Serve with plain basmati rice or naan bread.

QuickCook

Entertaining

Recipes listed by cooking time

10

30 Bouillabaisse

Serves 4

¼ cup olive oil
1 onion, diced
1 celery stick, diced
1 large fennel bulb, sliced
5 garlic cloves, crushed
½ teaspoon ground coriander
½ teaspoon cayenne
13½ oz can diced tomatoes
1 bouquet garni
pinch of saffron threads
4¼ pints (8½ cups) fish stock
4 lb nonoily fish fillets and shellfish
    of your choice
6 tablespoons mayonnaise
1 roasted red pepper
salt and pepper
slices of lightly toasted baguette,
    to serve

· Heat the oil in a large saucepan over low heat. Add the onion, celery, fennel, and 4 of the garlic cloves and gently cook for 7 minutes, or until softened. Stir in the ground coriander and cayenne and cook for a couple of seconds, then add the tomatoes, bouquet garni, saffron, and stock and bring to a boil. Season with salt and pepper, reduce the heat, and leave to simmer for 10 minutes.

· Add any firmer-fleshed fish first, such as monkfish and langoustines, and cook for 5 minutes. Add any remaining fish or shellfish and simmer for a further 5 minutes, or until cooked through. Discard any shellfish that remains closed.

· Pulse together the remaining crushed garlic clove with the mayonnaise and red pepper. Drizzle on the baguette and serve alongside the stew.

 Garlicky Shrimp Couscous

Cook 1 sliced garlic clove in a little olive oil for 2 minutes. Add 1¾ cups couscous, 1½ cups hot vegetable stock with a pinch of saffron, and 7 oz cooked peeled shrimp. Cover and stand for 5–7 minutes, then stir in ¾ cup sliced cherry tomatoes and some chopped parsley. Mix together the garlic, mayonnaise, and red pepper as above and drizzle onto the shrimp and coucous to serve.

 Clam Soup with Garlicky Mayonnaise

Heat 2 tablespoons olive oil in a saucepan over medium heat. Add 1 diced onion and cook for 5 minutes, or until softened. Pour in 4¾ cups water, 1¼ cups diced tomatoes, and a pinch of saffron threads. Leave to simmer for 7 minutes. Add 5 oz soup pasta along with 1 lb cleaned live clams and simmer, covered, for about 5 minutes until the clams have opened and the pasta is cooked through. Discard any clams that remain closed. Meanwhile, in a food processor, pulse together ¼ cup plus 2 tablespoons mayonnaise, 1 roasted red pepper from a jar, and 1 crushed garlic clove. Drizzle the mixture over the soup to serve.

30 Crispy Rice Paper Salmon Parcels with Soy Dressing

Serves 4

3 tablespoons rice vinegar
3 tablespoons soy sauce
1 tablespoon rice wine
1 tablespoon superfine sugar
4 large rice paper wrappers
4 thin skinless salmon fillets,
  weighing about 3 oz each
4 cilantro sprigs
1 tablespoon vegetable oil
2 scallions, sliced
salt and pepper

To serve

steamed rice
cooked edamame (soy) beans

- Mix together the vinegar, soy sauce, rice wine, and sugar. Dip each rice paper wrapper into a bowl of very hot water for 30 seconds, or until softened. Brush a little of the soy mixture over each salmon fillet Arrange a cilantro sprig in the center of each wrapper, then place a salmon fillet on top, presentation-side down, and season with salt and pepper.. Fold over the edges of the wrapper to make a parcel. Repeat with the remaining salmon fillets.

- Heat the vegetable oil in a large, nonstick skillet. Brush the parcels with a little water, then cook for 4 minutes on each side until golden and crisp and the fish is cooked through.

- Stir the scallion through the remaining soy dressing. Drizzle the mixture onto the fish and serve with steamed rice and edamame (soy) beans.

---

10 Salmon and Cilantro Parcels

Cut 4 x 3 oz thin skinless salmon fillets into thick strips. Dip the same number of small rice paper wrappers as salmon strips into a bowl of very hot water for 30 seconds, or until softened. Place on damp paper towels. Set a cilantro sprig and salmon strip in the center of each wrapper and roll up. Heat ¼ cup vegetable oil in a large skillet. Cook the parcels for 2–3 minutes, turning occasionally, until golden and crisp all over. Serve with soy sauce for dipping.

20 Salmon Teriyaki Egg Rolls

Brush 5 tablespoons teriyaki sauce all over 2 x 6 oz salmon fillets and drizzle with a little vegetable oil. Cook under a hot broiler for 3–5 minutes on each side. Leave to cool a little, then discard the skin and break into flakes. Mix together with 1 finely grated carrot, 1 minced scallion and ½ cup bean sprouts. Place heaped spoonfuls on egg roll wrappers, then fold over and roll up like a cigar. Mix together 1 tablespoon each cornstarch and water. Brush along the ends of the wrappers to secure. Fill a large, deep saucepan over medium heat one-third full with vegetable oil over medium heat. When a cube of bread dropped in the oil turns brown in 30 seconds the oil is ready. Deep-fry the egg rolls in batches for 3–5 minutes, or until golden. Drain the cooked egg rolls on paper towels and keep them warm while you cook the rest Serve with extra teriyaki sauce for dipping.

Lemon Sole with Pea Puree and Prosciutto

Serves 4

1 tablespoon butter
2 tablespoons olive oil
2 shallots, minced
1 potato, peeled and diced
scant ½ cup fresh fish stock
leaves from 1 thyme sprig
1 bay leaf
2 tablespoons light cream
2 cups frozen peas
4 slices of prosciutto
4 lemon sole fillets, weighing
   about 6 oz each
all-purpose flour, for dusting
lemon juice, to taste
salt and pepper

- Heat the butter and 1 tablespoon of the oil in a saucepan. Add the shallots and cook for 5 minutes until softened. Add the potato, stock, and herbs and simmer for 10 minutes until the potato is just cooked through. Remove the herbs and add the cream and peas. Cook for 3 minutes until just tender.

- Meanwhile, heat the remaining oil in a large, nonstick skillet. Add the prosciutto and cook for 1–2 minutes on each side until golden. Drain on paper towels. Season the sole fillets, dust with flour, and cook for 3–5 minutes on each side until just cooked through.

- Scoop out a handful of peas from the pan with a slotted spoon and reserve. Pulse the remaining contents in a food processor until really smooth, then return with the whole peas to the pan. Season well with salt and pepper and add lemon juice to taste. Spoon the mixture onto serving plates, arrange the fish and prosciutto on top, and serve.

Pea Shoot, Parma Ham, and Shrimp Salad Heat 1 teaspoon olive oil in a nonstick skillet over medium heat. Add 3 slices of Parma ham and cook for 1–2 minutes on each side until crisp. Gently toss together 5 oz cooked peeled small shrimp, 3 cups pea shoots, 3 tablespoons olive oil, and 2–3 teaspoons fresh lemon juice. Crumble the Parma ham and scatter on top to serve.

Lemon Sole with Pea and Leek Risotto Heat 1 tablespoon butter and 1 tablespoon vegetable oil in a deep skillet. Add 1 sliced large leek and a splash of water. Cook for about 5 minutes, or until soft. Stir in 2 cups risotto rice until well coated. Pour in a scant ½ cup dry white wine and boil until reduced. Add 3¾ cups hot vegetable stock, a ladleful at a time, stirring and simmering after each addition until the stock is absorbed before adding the next ladleful. After about 15 minutes, when all the stock is absorbed and the rice is nearly cooked, add 1 cup frozen peas. Cook for a further 5 minutes. Meanwhile, heat 1 tablespoon olive oil in a large, nonstick skillet. Season 4 x 6 oz lemon sole fillets, dust with flour, and cook for 2–3 minutes on each side until cooked through. Stir 2 tablespoons butter into the risotto. Scatter with chopped chives and serve with the fish.

30 Crab Cakes with Chipotle Salsa

Serves 4

1 egg, beaten
¼ cup mayonnaise
2 scallions, diced
1 teaspoon Worcestershire sauce
1 lb white crabmeat
1 cup dried bread crumbs
2 tablespoons vegetable oil
salt and pepper

For the chipotle salsa

4 tomatoes, diced
1 tablespoon minced onion
1–2 teaspoons minced chipotle
  chiles in adobo sauce or Tabasco
  sauce, to taste
1 tablespoon olive oil
1 lime
handful of cilantro, chopped

- Mix together the egg, mayonnaise, scallions, and Worcestershire sauce. Carefully stir in the crab, trying not to break it up, then season with salt and pepper. Lightly wet your hands, then shape the mixture into 12 small crab cakes.

- Pour the bread crumbs onto a plate, then coat the crab cakes in the crumbs. Place on a baking pan lined with parchment paper and place in the freezer for 10 minutes to firm up a little.

- Heat 1 tablespoon of the oil in a large, nonstick skillet. Cook half the crab cakes for 3 minutes on each side until brown. Remove from the pan and keep warm in the oven while you cook the remaining crab cakes in the same way.

- Meanwhile, for the salsa, mix together the tomatoes, onion, chiles or Tabasco, and oil. Add the finely grated zest of half the lime and a good squeeze of the juice, then season. Stir in the cilantro just before serving with the crab cakes.

---

10 Crab, Pepper, and Chipotle Dip

In a food processor, pulse together 1 roasted red pepper, 1 teaspoon chipotle in adobo sauce or Tabasco sauce to taste, 3 tablespoons mayonnaise, and generous ½ cup cream cheese until smooth. Stir in 7 oz white crabmeat. Heat gently in a small saucepan for 1–2 minutes. Serve with crackers for dipping.

20 Creamy Crab and Chipotle Pasta

Cook 13 oz dried spaghetti according to the package instructions. Meanwhile, heat 1 tablespoon olive oil in a skillet. Add 1 minced onion and cook for 5–7 minutes, or until softened. Add ¼ cup dry white wine and boil until reduced. Stir in 1 scant CUP crème fraîche and 1–2 teaspoons finely chopped chipotle chiles in adobo sauce or Tabasco sauce to taste, then add 1 lb white crabmeat. Drain the pasta and return it to the pan. Add the crab mixture and toss to coat the pasta, then stir in some chopped cilantro to serve.

3️ Smoked Haddock Soufflés

Serves 4

1¾ cups milk

14½ oz smoked haddock fillet

¼ cup plus 1 tablespoon butter

2 tablespoons finely grated
Parmesan cheese

½ cup all-purpose flour

generous ½ cup grated Gruyère
cheese

6 eggs, separated

2 sliced scallions

- Add the milk to the haddock in a shallow saucepan. Simmer for 7–10 minutes, or until the fish flakes easily. Pour the milk through a strainer into a jug. When the fish is cool enough to handle, tear it into flakes, discarding the skin and any bones.

- Meanwhile, grease 4 individual soufflé dishes well with some of the butter and dust with the grated Parmesan. Place the dishes on a baking pan. Melt the remaining butter in a saucepan over low heat. Add the flour and cook for 2 minutes. Slowly whisk in the poaching milk until smooth. Bring to a boil, whisking, and when it starts to bubble and thicken, remove from the heat and stir in the grated Gruyère and fish flakes. Stir in the egg yolks, one at a time, then leave to cool a little.

- Whisk the egg whites in a grease-free bowl until stiff and glossy. Stir one-third into the fish mixture, then carefully fold in the remaining mixture in 2 batches along with the scallions. Spoon into the soufflé dishes. Place in a preheated oven at 400°F for 10–12 minutes, or until well risen. Serve immediately.

 ### Smoked Salmon Carbonara

Cook 1 lb fresh linguine according to the package instructions. Meanwhile, mix together 1 egg and ¼ cup plus 1 tablespoon crème fraîche. Drain the pasta and return it to the pan. Add the egg mixture and toss until well combined. Stir in 5 oz smoked salmon, cut into strips. Scatter the pasta with some chopped chives to serve.

 ### Smoked Trout Puffs

In a food processor, pulse together ¾ cup all-purpose flour, 2 eggs, 1¼ cups milk and a good pinch of salt until you have a smooth batter. Carefully grease a 12-hole muffin pan well. Shred 10 oz skinless smoked trout fillets into flakes and place a little in each hole of the muffin pan. Divide the batter between the holes and scatter 2 sliced scallions over the tops. Place in a preheated oven at 425°F for 15 minutes, or until puffed and golden.

Fruits de Mer with Herb Aïoli

20

Serves 4

1 cup dry white wine
1 cup fish stock
1 bay leaf
2 raw lobster claws
4 raw crab claws
¼ lb raw small shrimp, shells on
8 langoustines
12 cleaned live clams
12 cleaned live mussels
4 oysters

For the herb aïoli

2 egg yolks
1–2 teaspoons fresh lemon juice
2 garlic cloves, crushed
1 scant cup olive oil
large handful of flat-leaf parsley,
  chopped
small handful of basil, chopped
salt and pepper

- Bring the wine and stock with the bay leaf to a boil in a deep skillet. Reduce to a simmer and add the lobster claws. Poach for 5 minutes. Remove from the pan with a slotted spoon and either keep warm or set aside to cool.

- Add the crab claws, shrimp, and langoustines and cook for 4 minutes, then remove as before. Add the clams and mussels and cook for about 4 minutes, or until they have opened. Discard any that remain closed. Use the stock for making a seafood risotto or soup.

- To make the aïoli, pulse together the egg yolks, lemon juice, and garlic cloves in a small food processor until well combined. With the motor running, slowly start to add the oil in a thin stream until the mixture starts to thicken, then add the remainder a little more quickly. Season with salt and pepper, then stir in the herbs, and spoon into a serving bowl.

- Open the oysters and arrange with the rest of the seafood on a platter. Serve with the aïoli.

10 **Fruits de Mer Rolls**
Mix 6 tablespoons mayonnaise with a handful of basil and flat-leaf parsley, chopped, the meat from the tail of a cooked lobster, and a generous ½ cup white crabmeat. Split open 4 soft white dinner rolls, fill with the seafood, mixture, some salad leaves, and a little lemon juice to serve.

30 **Fruits de Mer with Sauce Trio**
Prepare the fruits de mer and a half quantity of the herb aïoli as above. For a vinegar dipping sauce, mix together 1 minced shallot and ¼ cup red wine vinegar. For a Bloody Mary sauce, stir together ¼ cup tomato ketchup, 1 diced tomato, 3 tablespoons vodka, 2 teaspoons horseradish sauce, and ½ teaspoon each Worcestershire sauce and Tabasco sauce. Serve alongside the aïoli to accompany the fruits de mer.

 # Smoked Salmon and Beet Salad with Creamy Dressing

Serves 2

3½ oz cooked fresh beets, quartered

3 oz cups beet leaves or baby spinach

3½ oz smoked salmon slices crusty brown bread, to serve (optional)

For the creamy dressing

½ teaspoon white wine vinegar

2 tablespoons mayonnaise

2 tablespoons sour cream

1–3 teaspoons horseradish sauce

salt and pepper

- Whisk together all the dressing ingredients, then season well with salt and pepper.

- Arrange the remaining ingredients on serving plates, then drizzle with the dressing. Serve immediately with slices of crusty brown bread, if you like.

 2 Salmon and Beets with Creamy Dressing Heat 2 teaspoons olive oil in a nonstick skillet. Add 2 salmon fillets, skin-side up, and cook for 3 minutes, or until golden. Transfer, skin-side down, to a lightly oiled baking pan and place in a preheated oven at 400°F for about 10 minutes, or until the salmon is cooked through. After 5 minutes add 3½ oz ready-cooked fresh beets, cut into wedges, to the baking pan and return to the oven.

Meanwhile, prepare the dressing as above. Toss with 4 cups fresh spinach. Serve with the salmon and beets.

3 Salmon Carpaccio with Creamy Dressing Seal a 7 oz piece of salmon fillet in plastic wrap, then place in the freezer for 20 minutes to firm up. Using a very sharp knife, thinly slice the fish, cutting down on an angle to create thin slivers. Arrange on serving plates. Cut 3½ oz ready-cooked fresh beets into matchsticks and arrange on top. Prepare the dressing as above and drizzle onto everything to serve.

Chinese Banquet Sea Bass

Serves 4

1½ lb whole sea bass, gutted and scaled

¼ cup Shaoxing wine

¼ cup soy sauce

2 inch piece fresh ginger root, peeled and cut into matchsticks

2 teaspoons sesame oil

2 tablespoons vegetable oil

3 scallions, sliced

salt and pepper

- Set the fish on a heatproof plate, then season the cavity with salt and pepper. Pour 1 tablespoon of the Shaoxing wine and soy sauce onto the fish and place 1 tablespoon of the ginger on top. Place inside a steamer or covered wok with a rack and steam over simmering water for 15 minutes, or until the fish is cooked through. Remove the ginger and discard the cooking water.

- Heat the oils in a small saucepan. Meanwhile, arrange the scallions and remaining ginger on top of the fish. Pour the hot oil over the fish. Add the remaining rice wine and soy sauce to the pan and heat through briefly, then pour this over the fish as well. Serve immediately.

 Chinese Stir-Fried Sea Bass

Cut 4 x 6 oz sea bass fillets, skin on, into pieces. Dust all over with cornstarch. Heat 3 tablespoons vegetable oil in a wok on high heat and stir-fry the fish for 5 minutes, or until crisp and cooked through. Remove from the wok, add more oil if necessary, and stir-fry 2 sliced scallions, 1 sliced garlic clove, and 1 tablespoon chopped fresh ginger root for 2 minutes. Add 1 tablespoon each soy sauce and Shaoxing wine. Return the fish to the pan and stir to coat in the liquid. Scatter with chopped cilantro to serve.

 Marinated Chinese Sea Bass Fillets

Mix together 2 teaspoons diced fresh ginger root, 2 crushed garlic cloves, 1 thinly sliced shallot, and 6 tablespoons soy sauce. Pour the mixture onto 4 x 6 oz thin skinless sea bass fillets and leave to marinate for 10 minutes. Place each fillet on a piece of foil and spoon some of the marinade onto each. Fold the foil over tightly to seal, leaving a little air around the fish. Place on a baking sheet in a preheated oven at 400°F for 15 minutes, or until the fish is just cooked through. Meanwhile, heat 1 tablespoon vegetable oil in a skillet and gently cook 2 tablespoons sesame seeds until lightly browned. Scatter them onto the fish to serve.

30 Confit Salmon with Watercress Salad

Serves 6

6 salmon fillets, weighing about
 3½ oz each
2 teaspoons salt
finely grated zest of 1 lemon
2½ cups olive oil
12 garlic cloves
3 thyme sprigs
1 tablespoon white wine vinegar
3 tablespoons extra virgin olive oil
4 cups watercress
salt and pepper

- Season the salmon with the salt and then rub it all over with the lemon zest. Leave to marinate for 10 minutes.

- Take a roasting pan large enough to fit the salmon fillets snugly in one layer and cover the bottom with olive oil. Place the salmon fillets, skin-side down, in the pan. Pour the remaining olive oil all over the fish—it should just cover them. (If it doesn't, you will need to baste the fish a couple of times during cooking.) Tuck the garlic cloves and thyme sprigs around the fish and cover with foil.

- Place in a preheated oven at 275°F for 15 minutes, or until the fish is just cooked through.

- Whisk together the vinegar and extra virgin olive oil, then season well with salt and pepper. Toss the dressing with the watercress. Lift the salmon out of the oil and drain on paper towels. Serve 2 roasted garlic cloves per person with the watercress salad.

 Salmon with Watercress Pesto

Rub some olive oil onto 6 x 4 oz salmon fillets. Cook, skin-side up, under a preheated hot broiler for 5 minutes. Turn the fish over and cook for a further 3–5 minutes, or until cooked through. Meanwhile, in a food processor, pulse together 3½ cups watercress, 3 tablespoons toasted hazelnuts, ½ red chile, and 5 tablespoons extra virgin olive oil. Serve with the fish.

 Smoked Salmon Watercress Frittata

Heat 1 tablespoon olive oil in a nonstick skillet. Cook 1 diced onion for 5 minutes until softened. Whisk together 5 eggs and 2 tablespoons milk, then stir in 2 cups roughly chopped watercress. Remove the skillet from the heat and pour in the egg mixture. Take 2 x 3½ oz skinless hot-smoked salmon fillets, discard the skins, tear the flesh into chunks, and stir it into the skillet. Return the skillet to low heat and cook for 10 minutes, or until set. Finish the frittata off under the broiler to set the top, making sure you turn the handle away from the heat if it is not flameproof.

30 Crispy Parma Ham-Wrapped Monkfish

Serves 4

12 slices of Parma ham
1¼ lb piece of skinless monkfish
   fillet, boned and cut into 2 fillets
2 tablespoons toasted pine nuts
3 tablespoons drained capers
¼ cup extra virgin olive oil, plus
   extra for oiling
juice of 1 lemon
handful of flat-leaf parsley,
   chopped
salt and pepper

- Arrange the Parma ham slices slightly overlapping on a piece of waxed paper. Place 1 monkfish fillet on top and lightly season with salt and pepper. Lay the other fillet on top, the thin end facing the thick end to make a uniform-sized piece of fish. Use the waxed paper to roll the Parma ham around the fish and then slide them onto a lightly oiled baking pan.

- Place under a preheated hot broiler and cook for 10 minutes, then turn the parcel over and cook for a further 7–10 minutes, or until the fish is cooked through and the Parma ham is crisp. The fish is cooked when the tip of a metal skewer inserted in the center comes out warm. Meanwhile, mix together the remaining ingredients.

- Cut the monkfish into thick pieces and serve drizzled with the sauce.

 Crispy Pancetta and Scallops

Heat 1 tablespoon olive oil in a large skillet. Cut 12 slices of pancetta into thin strips. Cook for 1 minute, or until starting to brown. Add 12 cleaned plump scallops. Cook for 2–3 minutes on each side until browned and cooked through and the pancetta is crisp. Transfer to a serving plate. Add ¼ cup water and 1–2 teaspoons fresh lemon juice to the pan. Boil for 1 minute. Stir in 3 tablespoons fresh green pesto and ¼ cup crème fraîche. Drizzle the mixture onto the scallops and pancetta and serve.

 Crispy Parma Ham with Monkfish

Heat 2 tablespoons olive oil in a large skillet. Cut a 13 oz piece of skinless monkfish fillet into small medallions and cook on one side for 5 minutes, or until golden. Turn the fish over and spread a little fresh green pesto onto each medallion then scatter them evenly with ¼ cup bread crumbs and 2 tablespoons chopped pine nuts. Drizzle with a little more oil. Place the pan under a preheated hot broiler, making sure you turn the pan handle away from the heat if it is not flameproof, and cook for a

further 3–5 minutes, or until golden and just cooked through. Keep warm. Heat a small, dry skillet and cook 4 slices of Parma ham for 1–2 minutes on each side, or until crisp. Place the monkfish medallions on serving plates, then crumble the Parma ham into large pieces and scatter them over the fish to serve.

Chile Crab

Serves 4

2 tablespoons vegetable oil

1¼ lb raw crab claws

3 garlic cloves, crushed

1 tablespoon minced fresh ginger root

2–3 red chiles, seeded (optional) and minced

1¼ cups canned diced tomatoes

1 tablespoon soy sauce

1 tablespoon Shaoxing wine

1 tablespoon soft brown sugar

2 teaspoons rice vinegar or apple cider vinegar

2 teaspoons cornstarch

1 tablespoon water

2 scallions, shredded

plain rice, to serve

- Heat the oil in a large wok or skillet over high heat. Add the crab claws and cook for about 2 minutes, or until bright red. Remove them from the pan and set aside. Add the garlic and ginger and stir-fry for 30 seconds, then add the chiles followed by the tomatoes, soy sauce, Shaoxing wine, sugar, and vinegar. Simmer for 10 minutes, adding a little water if it seems necessary.

- Return the crab to the pan and cook for a further 5 minutes, or until cooked through. Mix together the cornstarch and measurement water until smooth. Stir into the pan and cook for 1 minute until the sauce is slightly thickened. Scatter with the scallions and serve with plain rice.

Sweet and Sour Chile Crab

Heat 2 tablespoons vegetable oil in a large wok or skillet. Stir-fry 3 crushed garlic cloves and 1 tablespoon minced fresh ginger root for 30 seconds. Add 1 lb ready-cooked crab claws, 2 tablespoons each tomato ketchup, sweet chili sauce, and water and a pinch of sugar. Heat through. Squeeze in some fresh lime juice to taste and scatter with chopped cilantro to serve.

Chile Coconut Crab Curry

Heat 1 tablespoon vegetable oil in a large wok or skillet over medium heat. Add 1 diced onion and cook for 5 minutes, or until softened. Stir in 2 crushed garlic cloves, 1 tablespoon minced fresh ginger root, and 1–2 minced chiles and cook for a further minute. Stir in 1 teaspoon each ground coriander and cumin, then add 2 lemon grass stalks and 1 fresh lime leaf. Pour in 1 scant cup coconut milk and ½ scant cup water. Leave to simmer for 10 minutes. Add 2 diced tomatoes and 1¼ lb raw crab claws and cook for 10 minutes, or until the crab is cooked through. Fish out and discard the lemon grass and lime leaf, then scatter the dish with chopped cilantro to serve.

30 Shrimp and Leek Pot Pies

Serves 4

12 oz sheet puff pastry
1 egg yolk, lightly beaten
2 tablespoons butter
1 tablespoon olive oil
2 leeks, thinly sliced
1 tablespoon all-purpose flour
¾ cup chicken stock
½ cup dry white wine
13 oz raw peeled jumbo shrimp
¾ cup light cream
1–2 teaspoons fresh lemon juice
salt and pepper

- Use an 8 oz ramekin to cut 4 rounds from the puff pastry, making each one ½ inch larger all around than the ramekin. Place the rounds on a cookie sheet and brush them all over with beaten egg yolk. Bake in a preheated oven at 425°F for 15–20 minutes, or until golden and crisp.

- Meanwhile, heat the butter and oil in a saucepan. Add the leeks and a splash of water and cook for 5–7 minutes, or until soft. Stir in the flour, then add the stock and wine. Leave to simmer for 7 minutes, or until the liquid has nearly boiled off. Add the shrimp and cook for 3 minutes, or until cooked through, then stir in the cream and cook for a further 1–2 minutes until heated through. Season with salt and pepper, and add the lemon juice.

- Divide the mixture between 4 x 8 oz ramekins. Set a pastry lid on top of each and serve

---

 ### Shrimp Dip with Toast

Cut off the crusts of 6 thick slices white bread. Cut each widthwise in half to make 2 thin slices. Place under a hot broiler and toast for 1–2 minutes on each side, or until golden and slightly curled. Cool a little. In a small food processor, pulse together 1¼ cups cream cheese and 5 oz cooked peeled shrimp to a chunky paste. Add a little fresh lemon juice, dust with some paprika, and serve with the toast.

 ### Upside-Down Shrimp Puffs

Use a 2 inch round cookie cutter to cut out 4 rounds from a 12 oz sheet puff pastry. Set them on a baking pan and brush them all over with lightly beaten egg. Place in a preheated oven at 425°F for 15 minutes, or until golden and crisp. Meanwhile, heat 2 tablespoons butter and 1 tablespoon olive oil in a saucepan. Add 2 sliced scallions and cook for 3 minutes, or until softened. Stir in ¼ cup dry white wine and cook until nearly boiled off. Stir through 7 oz cooked peeled jumbo shrimp and 6 tablespoons crème fraîche and heat through. Place the pastry rounds on serving plates and spoon the shrimp mixture on top. Scatter with chopped chives before serving.

3️ Baked Turbot with a Buttery Tarragon Sauce

Serves 4

1 tablespoon butter
3 lb whole turbot, gutted
½ lemon, sliced
3 tarragon sprigs
1 bay leaf
scant ½ cup dry white wine
salt and pepper

For the sauce

1 shallot, minced
1 tablespoon white wine vinegar
1½ tablespoons dry white wine
about ½ cup cold butter, cubed
handful of tarragon, chopped

- Grease a baking pan with a little of the butter, then place the fish on top, dark skin-side up. Place the lemon slices and herbs in the cavity, then pour the wine on top, dot the skin with the remaining butter, and season. Loosely cover with a sheet of waxed or parchment paper and place in a preheated oven at 400°F for 20–25 minutes, until just cooked through.

- Meanwhile, to make the sauce, place the shallot, vinegar, and wine in a saucepan and boil until reduced to 2 tablespoons. Whisking constantly, add the butter, a cube at a time, until the sauce thickens and turns creamy. Season with salt and pepper, add a little extra butter if it seems too sharp, and stir in the tarragon.

- Serve the tarragon sauce alongside the baked turbot.

 Shrimp Pasta with Tarragon Butter

Cook 1 lb fresh linguine according to the package instructions with ½ lb raw peeled jumbo shrimp (the shrimp will need about 3 minutes to cook through). Meanwhile, mix together 2 tablespoons softened butter, ¼ cup grated Parmesan cheese, 1–2 teaspoons fresh lemon juice, and a handful of tarragon, chopped. Drain the pasta and shrimp, reserving some of the cooking water. Stir the butter mixture into the pasta, along with a little of the cooking water to loosen, and serve.

 Broiled Cod with Tarragon Butter

Boil ¼ cup dry white wine in a saucepan until reduced to 1 tablespoon and set aside to cool. Mix together with 3½ tablespoons softened butter, a handful of tarragon, chopped, and a little finely grated lemon zest. Brush a little olive oil over 4 x 5 oz cod fillets. Cook, skin-side up, under a preheated hot broiler for 5–7 minutes, or until browned and crisp. Turn over and cook for a further 3 minutes. Dot the butter mixture all over each piece of fish. Broil for 2 minutes longer then serve immediately.

30 Hot-Smoked Salmon Kedgeree with Quails' Eggs

Serves 4

3 tablespoons boiling water

pinch of saffron threads

1 tablespoon vegetable oil

2 tablespoons butter

1 onion, minced

1 garlic clove, minced

1 teaspoon finely grated fresh
   ginger root

1 teaspoon mild curry powder

1¼ cups basmati rice

3¼ cups fish or vegetable stock

6 quails' eggs

10 oz hot-smoked salmon fillets,
   skinned

5 tablespoons crème fraîche

salt and pepper

chopped flat-leaf parsley, to
   garnish

- Pour the measurement water over the saffron in a bowl and leave to infuse. Meanwhile, heat the oil and butter in a large saucepan. Add the onion and gently cook for 5 minutes, or until softened. Stir in the garlic and ginger and cook for a further 1 minute. Add the curry powder followed by the rice and stir until well coated.

- Add the stock and saffron with its soaking liquid. Bring to a boil, then leave to simmer for 15 minutes.

- Meanwhile, boil the quails' eggs in a saucepan of boiling water for 3 minutes. Drain and cool under cold running water. Remove and discard the shells and halve the eggs.

- Break the salmon into flakes and add to the rice with the egg halves. Remove from the heat, cover, and leave to stand for 5 minutes to warm through. Gently stir in the crème fraîche and season with salt and pepper. Spoon onto plates and scatter with chopped parsley to serve.

 Eggs with Smoked Salmon Dippers

Bring a saucepan of water to a boil. Carefully lower in 4 hens' eggs and cook for 4 minutes for a runny yolk. Transfer the eggs to egg cups and remove the tops. Wrap thin strips of smoked salmon around 8 long bread sticks and use them to dunk in the egg yolks.

 Smoked Salmon Pasta with Eggs

Infuse a pinch of saffron threads in 3 tablespoons boiling water. Meanwhile, heat 1 tablespoon olive oil in a saucepan over medium heat and add 1 sliced shallot. Cook for 5 minutes and add ¾ cup dry white wine. Simmer for about 8 minutes, or until reduced. Add the saffron with its soaking liquid and ¼ cup light cream and heat through. While preparing the sauce, cook 13 oz dried spaghetti according to the package instructions. Bring a small pan of water to a boil. Stir the water to create a whirlpool and crack 1 egg into the center. Poach for 3-4 minutes, then remove with a slotted spoon and keep warm. Repeat with another 3 eggs. Drain the pasta, return it to the pan, and stir in the saffron sauce. Serve with the poached eggs on top and scattered with strips of smoked salmon.

30 Creamy Seafood Lasagne

Serves 4

10½ oz jar tomato pasta sauce

pinch of dried red pepper flakes

7 oz skinless cod fillet,
 cut into bite-size pieces

7 oz cooked peeled small shrimp

3½ oz ready-cooked shelled
 mussels

olive oil, for oiling

10 oz fresh lasagne sheets

1 scant cup crème fraîche

¼ cup plus 1 tablespoon milk

¼ cup grated Parmesan cheese

- Heat the tomato sauce in a small saucepan together with the dried red pepper flakes and cod until warmed through. Add the shrimp and mussels.

- Spread a little of the seafood mixture all over the bottom of a lightly oiled baking dish. Cover with a layer of lasagne sheets. Add half the remaining seafood mixture. Mix together the crème fraîche and milk to make a smooth sauce, then drizzle one-quarter over the ingredients in the baking dish. Cover with another layer of lasagne sheets Repeat until you have 3 layers of lasagne sheets, then pour the remaining crème fraîche sauce on the top and scatter with the Parmesan.

- Place in a preheated oven at 400°F for 15–20 minutes, or until golden and cooked through.

Creamy Shrimp and Tomato Linguine

Cook 1 lb fresh linguine according to the package instructions with 7 oz raw peeled jumbo shrimp (the shrimp will need about 3 minutes to cook through). Drain, return to the pan. Add ¾ cup halved cherry tomatoes, ¼ cup mascarpone cheese, and handful of chopped basil. Give it a good stir and serve.

Creamy Shrimp and Zucchini

Lasagne Heat ¾ cup dry white wine in a saucepan and simmer for about 10 minutes, or until reduced by half and syrupy. Stir in ½ lb raw peeled small shrimp and simmer for 3–5 minutes, or until they are pink and just cooked through. Meanwhile, use a vegetable peeler to slice 1 zucchini into long curls. Stir 1¼ cups crème fraîche into the shrimp until melted, followed by a little finely grated lemon zest. While the sauce is simmering, cook 12 dried lasagne sheets in a large saucepan of salted boiling water for 7 minutes, or until tender. Drain and return to the pan. Stir in a little of the sauce. Arrange on a serving plate with the zucchini curls and drizzle with the remaining sauce to serve.

2⃝ Lobster Thermidor

Serves 4

1 tablespoon butter
1 tablespoon olive oil
1 shallot, diced
3 tablespoons dry sherry
1 teaspoon Dijon mustard
scant ½ cup crème fraîche
2 small ready-cooked lobsters,
   weighing about 1 lb 5 oz each
½ cup grated Gruyère cheese
salt

- Heat the butter and oil in a small saucepan. Add the shallot and cook for 5 minutes, or until softened. Pour in the sherry and cook for 2 minutes, or until nearly boiled off. Whisk in the mustard and crème fraîche, heat through, and season with salt.

- Meanwhile, using a large knife, cut the lobsters lengthwise in half. Remove the meat from the tail and claws, reserving the main shell halves. Cut the lobster meat into large chunks.

- Add the lobster meat to the sauce and warm through. Carefully spoon the mixture into the tail cavities of the reserved lobster shell halves and scatter with the Gruyère. Cook under a preheated hot broiler for 3–5 minutes, or until golden and bubbling.

 Lobster with Thermidor Butter

Mix together 2 tablespoons softened butter, ¼ cup grated Parmesan cheese, 1 tablespoon crème fraîche, 1 teaspoon Dijon mustard, 1–2 teaspoons fresh lemon juice, and a pinch of paprika. Use a large knife to cut 2 x 1 lb 5 oz ready-cooked lobsters lengthwise in half. Remove the meat from the claws and tuck around the tail meat. Dot 1 tablespoon butter all over the surface. Cook under a preheated hot broiler for 3–5 minutes, or until golden and bubbling, then serve.

 Lobster in Rich Thermidor Sauce

Heat 2 tablespoons butter in a saucepan, stir in ¼ cup all-purpose flour and cook for 2 minutes. Slowly whisk in 1¼ cups milk until smooth. Bring to a boil, whisking, then simmer for a few minutes, or until thickened, then set aside and keep warm. Meanwhile, heat 1 tablespoon butter in a separate saucepan. Add 1 minced shallot and gently cook for 8 minutes, or until very soft. Cut 2 x 1 lb 5 oz ready-cooked lobsters lengthwise in half. Remove the meat from the tail and claws, reserving the main shell halves. Cut the lobster meat into large chunks. Pour a scant ½ cup dry white wine into the shallot pan and boil until reduced. Add to the sauce along with ¼ cup heavy cream and 2 egg yolks. Remove from the heat and mix together. Add the lobster meat with a handful of tarragon, chopped, 1–2 teaspoons fresh lemon juice, and a pinch of cayenne and spoon into the lobster shells. Scatter with ¼ cup grated Gruyère cheese. Cook under a hot broiler for 5 minutes, or until golden brown and bubbling.

30 Whole Roasted Salmon with Lemon and Herb Tartare

Serves 4–6

3 tablespoons olive oil
3 lb thick piece of salmon, cut into
  2 fillets
1 lemon, sliced
handful of mixed herbs, finely
  chopped
salt

For the sauce

¼ cup plus 2 tablespoons
  mayonnaise
2 teaspoons drained capers,
  roughly chopped
1 scallion, diced
1 teaspoon superfine sugar
1 teaspoon wholegrain mustard
lemon juice, to taste
handful of dill, chopped

- Brush a large baking pan with a little of the oil. Place 1 salmon fillet, skin-side down, on the prepared pan and season with a little salt. Arrange the lemon slices and herbs on top. Season the other fillet and place on top, skin-side up.

- Tie pieces of kitchen string around the salmon to secure. Drizzle over the remaining oil. Place in a preheated oven at 425°F for 25 minutes, or until just cooked through.

- Meanwhile, mix together the sauce ingredients and place in a serving bowl. Serve alongside the fish with some buttered new potatoes and asparagus.

 Caper and Lemon Salmon Strips

Mix together 1 tablespoon finely chopped capers, ¼ cup mayonnaise, and a little grated lemon zest. Cut a 13 oz skinless salmon fillet into thin strips. Place on a lightly oiled baking pan. Spread the mayonnaise thickly on top of each strip. Scatter evenly with ¼ cup dried bread crumbs. Place under a preheated hot broiler for 5 minutes until cooked through.

 Salmon with Preserved Lemon

Mix together 1 teaspoon each ground cumin, paprika, and diced preserved lemon, a handful of cilantro, chopped, and 2 tablespoons olive oil. Make slits in the skin of 4 x 5 oz salmon fillets. Rub the spice mix all over and inside of the slits. Set aside to marinate for 5–10 minutes. Heat a ridged griddle pan until smoking hot. Cook the salmon, skin-side down, for 4–5 minutes, then turn the fish over and cook for a further 3 minutes, or until cooked through. Sprinkle the fish with 1–2 teaspoons fresh lemon juice and serve with some couscous and a tomato salad.

Pan-Fried Sole with Butter and Lemon

Serves 2

¼ cup plus 2 tablespoons butter
2 tablespoons all-purpose flour
2 gutted whole sole or flounder,
   weighing about 14½ oz each
handful of mixed herbs including
   parsley, chopped
juice of ½ lemon
salt

- Heat ¼ cup plus 1 tablespoon butter in a small saucepan over low heat until melted, then skim off and discard the foam that forms on the top. Pour the clear melted butter into a bowl, leaving behind and discarding the milky solids at the bottom of the pan.

- Season the flour with salt, then dust the fish all over with the seasoned flour. Heat 1 very large or 2 smaller skillets over medium-high heat and add the clarified butter from the bowl. Place the fish in the pan and cook for 3 minutes. Carefully turn the fish over and cook for a further 4 minutes, or until just cooked through. Place on serving plates.

- Wipe the pan clean with paper towels. Add the remaining 1 tablespoon butter to the pan and heat until melted. Remove from the heat, stir in the herbs and drizzle the mixture over the fish with the lemon juice. Serve immediately.

Sole Goujons with Butter and Capers

Discard the skin of 2 x ½ lb sole fillets and cut into strips ½ inch thick. Dust the strips all over with all-purpose flour. Heat 3 tablespoons olive oil in a skillet and cook for 5 minutes, turning once, until just cooked through. Wipe the pan clean with paper towels. Add 2 tablespoons butter and heat until melted, then add 1 tablespoon drained capers and cook for 1 minute. Spoon the mixture onto fish along with a little fresh lemon juice to serve.

Sole with Butter and Wine

Season 2 x 14½ oz gutted whole sole or flounder with salt. Place on a lightly greased baking pan. Dot the fish all over with about 3 tablespoons butter, drizzle with a little dry white wine, and scatter with the finely grated zest of ½ lemon. Place in a preheated oven at 400°F for 15 minutes, or until lightly browned and just cooked through.

Creamy Oysters and Mushrooms in Brioche Pots

Serves 4

¾ cup dry white wine
  or Champagne
2 shallots, minced
scant ½ cup heavy cream
2 tablespoons butter
2 slices pancetta (Italian bacon),
  cut into thin matchsticks
3 oz oyster mushrooms, halved if
  large
8 oysters, shucked (reserving
  the liquor)
4 individual brioche breads
handful of chives, finely chopped,
  plus extra to garnish (optional)

- Boil the wine or Champagne with the shallots in a saucepan until reduced by half. Add the cream and cook until you have a rich, creamy sauce.

- Heat 1 tablespoon of the butter in a skillet. Add the pancetta and cook for 2 minutes, or until turning golden, then add the mushrooms and cook for 3 minutes until browned all over. Add to the sauce with the oysters and their liquor and cook for 2 minutes.

- Meanwhile, slice the lid off each brioche and pull out most of the bread inside. Melt the remaining butter in a small saucepan and brush it all over the inside of the brioche. Place on a cookie sheet in a preheated oven at 400°F for 5–10 minutes, or until crisp.

- Stir the chives into the sauce, then spoon into the brioche pots, scatter with more chives, if you like, and serve.

 Creamy Broiled Oysters

Boil ¾ cup dry white wine with 2 minced shallots in a saucepan until reduced by half. Add a scant ½ cup heavy cream and cook until you have a rich, creamy sauce. Open 8 oysters and discard the flat top shells, leaving the oysters in the bottom shells. Place on a baking pan. Season the sauce, then pour a little over each oyster. Place under a preheated hot broiler and cook for 2 minutes, or until lightly browned, then scatter with some chopped chives before serving.

 Creamy Oyster Chowder

Heat 2 tablespoons butter in a saucepan. Add 1 minced onion and cook for about 8 minutes, or until very soft. Pour in ¾ cup dry white wine and boil until reduced. Stir in 1 diced potato and 1¼ cups each light cream, milk, and vegetable or fresh fish stock. Bring to a boil, then leave to simmer for 10–12 minutes, or until the potatoes are tender. Meanwhile, cook 4 slices smoked bacon until crisp. Shuck 16 oysters, add to the soup with their liquor, and cook for 2 minutes. Ladle the soup into bowls, crumble the bacon and scatter it, along with some chopped chives, onto the soup to serve.

3⦾ Citrus Scallop Ceviche

Serves 4

½ orange
1 lime
1 lb cleaned scallops, chopped
¾ cup cherry tomatoes, diced
1 tablespoon minced red onion
½ red chile, minced
handful of cilantro, chopped
2 tablespoons extra virgin olive oil
salt

- Remove the zest from the orange and lime with a zester. Squeeze the juice from the citrus fruits into a bowl and stir in the zest. Add the scallops and leave to marinate for 25 minutes.

- Toss the scallops with the tomatoes, onion, chile, and cilantro, then season with salt. Pile into scallop shells or serving dishes. Drizzle with the oil and serve.

 ### 1⦾ Citrus Griddled Scallops

Toss 1 lb cleaned scallops in 2 tablespoons vegetable oil. Heat a ridged griddle pan until smoking hot, add the scallops, and cook for 1–2 minutes on each side, or until just cooked through. Remove from the pan. Squeeze the juice of ½ lime and scatter 1 tablespoon orange juice onto the scallops, then toss them with ¾ cups diced cherry tomatoes, 1 tablespoon minced red onion, ½ red chile, minced, a handful of cilantro, chopped, and 2 tablespoons extra virgin olive oil. Season with salt before serving.

 ### 2⦾ Citrus Shrimp Tostadas

Fill a large, deep saucepan one-third full with vegetable oil over medium heat. When a cube of bread dropped into the oil turns brown in 15 seconds the oil is ready. Deep-fry 1 corn tortilla wrap for about 1½ minutes, or until golden and crispy. Drain on paper towels. Repeat with 3 more tortillas. Leave to cool. Mix together ¾ cup diced cherry tomatoes, 1 tablespoon minced red onion, ½ red chile, minced, a handful of cilantro, chopped, and the juice of ½ lime. Thinly slice ½ an iceberg lettuce and arrange on top of the tortillas. Slice 1 avocado into thin wedges and place on top of the lettuce. Scatter with the tomato mixture along with 7 oz cooked peeled jumbo shrimp. Evenly scatter ¼ cup grated cheddar cheese on top and add a spoonful of sour cream to serve.

3 Sea Bass Baked in a Salt Crust with Fennel Mayo

Serves 4

4 lb coarse sea salt

2 egg whites

3 lb whole sea bass, gutted but not scaled

½ fennel bulb, thinly sliced

1 lemon, thinly sliced

¼ cup plus 2 tablespoons mayonnaise

2 teaspoons crushed fennel seeds

1 tablespoon Pernod (optional)

- Mix together the salt and egg whites. Spread a layer of the salt mixture over the bottom of a roasting pan large enough to hold the whole fish. Place the fish on top and tuck the fennel and lemon slices inside the cavity. Completely cover the fish with the remaining salt mixture (don't worry if the tail is still exposed). Place in a preheated oven at 400°F for 25 minutes, or until cooked through.

- Meanwhile, whisk together the mayonnaise, crushed fennel seeds, and Pernod, if using.

- To serve, crack the salt crust by giving it a tap with the back of a knife, then lift the salt away. Pull the skin away from the fish, then slice into fillets and serve with the fennel mayo, some steamed baby new potatoes, and a tomato salad.

---

1 Shrimp Skewers with Chile Salt Dip

Seed, peel, and then slice a small mango into wedges. Thread onto skewers, alternating with 5 oz cooked peeled jumbo shrimp. Mix together 2 tablespoons coarse sea salt, 1 tablespoon sugar, and 1 minced red chile. Lightly dip the shrimp into the salt mixture before eating.

2 Caribbean Salt Fishcakes

Cook 5 oz salt fish in boiling water for 5 minutes, then drain and flake. Meanwhile, mince 3 scallions and 1 chile and chop the leaves from 1 thyme sprig. Mix this with the boiled fish, along with 2¼ cups flour and 1 tablespoon baking powder. Slowly stir in 1 cup milk and a scant ½ cup water to make a batter just thick enough to drop off of the spoon. Fill a deep saucepan one-third full with vegetable oil over medium heat. When a cube of bread dropped into the oil browns in 15 seconds the oil is ready. Carefully drop tablespoonfuls of the batter into the oil in batches. Fry for 2 minutes, drain, and serve.

Crispy Deep-Fried Seafood

Serves 4

¼ cup cornstarch
¼ cup fine polenta
vegetable oil, for deep-frying
¼ lb cleaned baby squid, cut into rings
¼ lb raw peeled jumbo shrimp
6 cleaned plump scallops, halved
¼ lb smelt, such as whitebait or rainbow smelt
salt and pepper
lemon wedges, to serve

- Mix together the cornstarch and polenta. Place in a large freezer bag and season well with salt and pepper. Cover a cookie sheet with a few layers of paper towels.

- Fill a large, deep saucepan over medium heat one-third full with oil. When a cube of bread dropped in the oil turns brown in 15 seconds the oil is ready. Add the squid to the freezer bag, seal, and shake well until coated. Shake off the excess cornstarch mixture and deep-fry the squid for about 3 minutes, or until just golden and cooked through. Place on the prepared cookie sheet to drain, and keep warm. Repeat, each in turn, with the shrimp, scallops, and fish. Serve with wedges of lemon.

 Crispy-Topped Broiled Squid

Pat 7 oz raw squid rings dry. Mix together the finely grated zest of 1 lemon, 1 teaspoon minced capers, and ¼ olive oil. Toss the squid rings into the mixture to coat. Arrange the squid in a single layer on a baking pan, then scatter ½ cup dried bread crumbs evenly on top of them and drizzle with a little more oil. Cook under a preheated hot broiler for 3–5 minutes, or until golden and just cooked through.

 Buttermilk-Marinated Crispy Squid Pour ¾ cup buttermilk into a bowl. Add 10 oz cleaned squid, cut into rings, and leave for 15 minutes to marinate. Mix together ¼ cup each cornstarch and fine polenta. Place in a large freezer bag and season well with salt and pepper. Fill a large, deep saucepan over medium heat one-third full with vegetable oil. When a cube of bread dropped in the oil turns brown in 15 seconds the oil is ready.

Add half the squid to the bag, seal, and shake well until coated. Shake the excess cornstarch mixture off of the squid rings and deep-fry for about 3 minutes, or until just golden. Drain on paper towels. Repeat with the remaining squid rings. Serve hot with lemon wedges on the side.

Clam Linguine in Chile Crème Fraîche Sauce

Serves 4

2 tablespoons olive oil
3 garlic cloves, sliced
½ red chile, minced
scant ½ cup dry white wine
2 lb cleaned live clams
1 lb fresh linguine
scant 1 cup crème fraîche
salt and pepper
handful of flat-leaf parsley,
   chopped, to garnish

- Heat the oil in a large saucepan over medium heat. Add the garlic and chile and fry for a few seconds. Pour in the wine and bring to a boil. Add the clams, then reduce the heat, cover the pan, and cook for 5 minutes, or until they have opened. Discard any that remain closed.

- Meanwhile, cook the pasta according to the package instructions. Drain, reserving some of the cooking water, and return to the pan.

- Stir the clams along with the crème fraîche into the pasta, adding a little of the reserved cooking water to loosen if necessary. Season with salt and pepper, then scatter with the parsley to serve.

 ### Clam Linguine Pasta Parcels

Cook 13 oz dried linguine for 3 minutes less than instructed on the package, drain, and return to the pan. Fry 3 crushed garlic cloves and ½ red chile, minced, briefly in 2 tablespoons olive oil. Stir in ¼ cup dry white wine and 1 scant cup crème fraîche, then add to the pasta and toss to coat. Divide the pasta among 4 pieces of lightly oiled foil. Divide 1 lb cleaned live clams among the pasta portions. Seal each tightly, leaving a little air around the clams. Place on a baking pan in a preheated oven at 400°F for 5–8 minutes, or until the clams have opened. Discard any that remain closed.

Spiced Clam Chowder

Heat 1 tablespoon butter and 1 tablespoon vegetable oil in a skillet. Add 3 slices smoked bacon, diced, and cook for 3–5 minutes, or until golden brown. Remove from the pan. Add 1 diced onion and cook for 7 minutes, or until softened. Stir in 1 minced chile and return the diced bacon to the pan. Pour in scant ½ cup dry white wine and boil for about 2 minutes until reduced. Pour in 2 cups milk and 1 scant cup each heavy cream and chicken stock and bring to a boil. Stir in ¾ lb baby potatoes, halved, and cook for 7 minutes. Add 1 lb cleaned live clams. Cover and cook for 5 minutes, or until the clams have opened. Discard any that remain closed. Scatter with a handful of flat-leaf parsley, chopped, to serve.

Shellfish and Tomato Bisque

Serves 4

1 lb shellfish shells
¼ cup plus 2 tablespoons butter
1 onion, diced
1 carrot, diced
1 celery stick, diced
1 tablespoon tomato paste
2 tablespoons brandy
¼ cup dry white wine
¾ cup diced tomatoes
3¼ pints (6¼ cups) fish stock
1 bay leaf
¼ cup white long-grain rice
scant ½ cup heavy cream
7 oz ready-cooked shellfish
salt and pepper
finely chopped tarragon, to
  garnish

- Chop up the shells as much as possible with a heavy knife. Heat the butter in a large saucepan over medium heat. Add the onion, carrot, celery, and shells and cook for about 5 minutes, or until the vegetables are softened, pressing down on the shells as much as you can. Stir in the tomato paste followed by the brandy. Cook until the brandy has evaporated, then add the wine and cook for 2 minutes, or until reduced.

- Add the tomatoes, stock, bay leaf, and rice. Bring to a boil, then simmer for about 15 minutes.

- Pour the mixture into a blender (discarding any very large shells) and pulse until the shells have broken up and are no larger than your fingernail. Pass the mixture through a fine strainer into a pan, pressing out as much juice as you can.

- Stir in the cream, season with salt and pepper, scatter with the cooked shellfish, and heat through. Ladle into bowls, garnish with finely chopped tarragon, and serve.

---

1 Crab and Tomato Salad

Mix together 2 tablespoons mayonnaise, 1 tablespoon sour cream, and 1–2 teaspoons fresh lemon juice. Arrange 3 large sliced tomatoes on a serving plate with some watercress sprigs. Scatter evenly with 1 cup white crabmeat. Spoon the dressing on top, scatter with chopped chives, and serve.

2 Crab and Tomato Soufflé Omelets

Separate 4 eggs. Stir the yolks together with a little seasoning. Whisk the whites in another bowl until soft peaks form. Stir the whites into the yolks in 3 batches. Heat 1 tablespoon butter in a small skillet. Add one-quarter of the egg mixture and cook for 1 minute, or until starting to set. Scatter with 2½ tablespoons white crabmeat and spoon on 1 tablespoon crème fraîche. Place the skillet under a preheated hot broiler, turning the pan handle away from the heat if not flameproof. Cook for 1–2 minutes until puffed and cooked through. Scatter with 1 sliced cherry tomato and fold the omelet over. Keep warm while you make the rest of the omelets.

FIS-ENTE-JAK

Index

Page references in *italics* indicate photographs

Acknowledgments

Recipes by **Emma Lewis**
Executive Editor **Eleanor Maxfield**
Senior Editor **Sybella Stephens**
Copy Editor **Jo Richardson**
Art Direction **Tracy Killick and Geoff Fennell**
    for Tracy Killick Art Direction and Design
Original design concept **www.gradedesign.com**
Designer **Ginny Zeal for Tracy Killick Art Direction and Design**
Photographer **William Shaw**
Home Economist **Emma Lewis**
Prop Stylist **Liz Hippisley**
Production **Lucy Carter**

The author would like to thank Walter Purkis of Muswell Hill,
London who, like many others, is a wonderful source of help
and advice for all things fishy.